VGM Opportunities Series

OPPORTUNITIES IN
CUSTOMER SERVICE CAREERS

Blanche Ettinger

Foreword by
William E. Waers
Manager
GE Answer Center

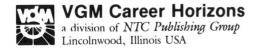 **VGM Career Horizons**
a division of *NTC Publishing Group*
Lincolnwood, Illinois USA

Cover Photo Credits:

Front cover: upper left, American Airlines; upper right and lower left, *Marketing News;* lower right, Lilian Vernon.

Back cover: upper left and lower right, *Marketing News;* upper right, DeVry, Inc.; lower left, Manpower Temporary Services.

Library of Congress Cataloging-in-Publication Data

Ettinger, Blanche.
    Opportunities in customer service careers / Blanche Ettinger.
        p.   cm. — (VGM opportunities series)

    Includes bibliographical references.
    ISBN 0-8442-8189-1 — ISBN 0-8442-8190-5 (pbk.)
    1. Customer service—Vocational guidance. I. Title. II. Series.
HF5415.5.E87   1992
658.8'12'023—dc20   92-23
                                                                CIP

Published by VGM Career Horizons, a division of NTC Publishing Group.
© 1992 by NTC Publishing Group, 4255 West Touhy Avenue,
Lincolnwood (Chicago), Illinois 60646-1975 U.S.A.
Manufactured in the United States of America.

2 3 4 5 6 7 8 9 0 VP 9 8 7 6 5 4 3 2 1

ABOUT THE AUTHOR

Blanche Ettinger is a professor in the Department of Secretarial and Office Information Systems at Bronx Community College of The City University of New York and an adjunct professor in the Business Education Program at New York University. She formerly taught on the high school level; prior to that, she was secretary to the executive vice-president of Cohn Hall Marx Company.

She received her B.A. and M.S. degrees from Hunter College of The City University of New York and an Ed.D. in business education from New York University, where she also took many courses in guidance and occupational information.

Doctor Ettinger has earned a national reputation for her many contributions to the field of business education. Through the years, she has been very active in professional organizations. She is a past president of the Business Education Association of Metropolitan New York, The New York State Association of Two-Year Colleges, Office Technology/Secretarial Educators of SUNY, and Alpha Xi Chapter of Delta Pi Epsilon (honorary graduate business education society). She is also a member of the Business Teachers Association of New York State, The

National Business Education Association, International Society of Business Education, and Phi Delta Kappa.

Dr. Ettinger was the 1982 recipient of the prestigious Delta Pi Epsilon National Research Award. Other honors bestowed on her include 1987 EBEA Educator-of-the-Year, 1987 Outstanding Member Award of The New York State Association of Two-Year Colleges, 1982 Paul S. Lomax Award (Alpha Chapter, New York University), 1979 Estelle L. Popham Award (Alpha Xi Chapter, Hunter College), and 1977 Certificate of Recognition (New York State Association of Two-Year Colleges). She is listed in *Who's Who in the East, Foremost Women of the Twentieth Century, Who's Who in American Education,* and *Who's Who in the World.*

Among her recent publications (some with co-authors) are: *Machine Transcription: Language Skills for Information Processing,* Second Edition (1992), *Opportunities in Secretarial Careers,* Second Edition (1992), "Stretching Students' Language Skills: A Multi-Faceted Approach," (1991), "Basic Skills and Core Competencies" (1989), *Keyboarding Proficiency Drillbook* (1988), *Time-It! Drillbook* (1988), and *Opportunities in Office Occupations,* Fourth Edition (1988).

In addition to authoring texts and articles, Dr. Ettinger is an educational consultant; conducts workshops; and is a guest speaker, moderator, and panelist at many institutions and at professional meetings throughout the nation.

FOREWORD

Today's customer environment is different from that of many years ago. Today, customers are more careful in their shopping, there is more interest in do-it-yourself repair, there are more working women, there is a rising quality expectation, and there is a desire for personal treatment. Exceeding customer expectations is one of the surest ways to guarantee success in business.

Research shows that customers want and expect major corporations to furnish information and interaction quickly and conveniently. Many corporations are perceived as somewhat "faceless" by the customer. Excellent customer service can put a "face" on the corporation.

What is customer service? It is everything that goes into meeting customers' needs, handling customer requests, surfacing and handling complaints, building their confidence and winning their loyalty.

The benefits a corporation can expect include increased sales and market share, reduced service costs, reduced product return, improved productivity, and enhancement of the corporation's public image.

The formula for success in customer service has a strong emphasis on people. The successful customer service professional must have good interpersonal skills, including empathy for the customer. Customer service pros are outgoing, enthusiastic, assertive, and persuasive. Your education will probably include courses in business, marketing, and communication. Customer service professionals will be expected to type 40 words per minute and operate a computer terminal. Excellent customer service organizations will provide employees with new hire training, on-going training, and reimbursement for continuing education.

Customer service is a diverse field. You may find yourself employed full time or part time in a variety of industries. You may be asked to work nontraditional hours because at many corporations customer service is provided 24 hours a day, 7 days a week. You may work in a sales, order processing, credit, marketing, or product service department. However you apply your customer service skills, your goal will remain the same: to provide that vital link between your company and its customers that ensures the continued success and satisfaction of both.

William E. Waers
Manager
GE Answer Center

PREFACE

Present economic conditions reflect the importance of customer service. Newspapers and TV news reports indicate daily the number of workers being released from their positions. Many employees who aren't being released are those in positions that deal with customer service, a field with a low attrition rate.

Opportunities in Customer Service Careers is a key source for knowledge about the growing field of customer service as a career. Quality in service, products, and operations has become the main focus in industry—for its survival. Firms that give quality in every aspect of their business will gain and retain customer loyalty, the basic criterion for any successful organization. Companies must meet their competition, and the only way to earn a perfect score is by actually giving superior service to its customers. Management has begun to realize that it is the customer who makes the difference! This means that specialized personnel are required to carry out the mission of these firms. This gives you the opportunity to enter a field that has great growth potential.

The jobs are diversified and require a varied set of skills, depending on the company goals, particular job, and organizational structure. You have the option of working for a small or large firm, in an urban or suburban area, and in an industry of your choice. This book has been written with you, the reader, in mind. You should be acquainted with information about customer service as a field of work, how it evolved, and the self-satisfaction that can be derived from employment in this field.

Opportunities in Customer Service Careers consists of eight chapters. In Chapter 1, you learn about the meaning and development of the customer-service concept. In Chapter 2, you are then exposed to the service cycle, the ways in which customer service is provided, and some strategies for understanding and dealing with customers. As the book progresses, in Chapters 3, 4, and 5, you gain some insight about different types of industries, the kinds of jobs that exist, and the demand for customer service personnel. You learn about the skills, knowledge, and personal traits needed for employment in this field. In Chapter 6, you will be enlightened about some programs of study that will prepare you for this career. If this is the field for you, then you will want to learn how to get ahead. This is discussed in Chapter 7. The last section should help you in preparing for and finding a job that can be enriching, challenging, and interesting.

Find out why you need to be a people-oriented person to be successful in this type of career. Discover a relatively new career path, enter it during its early stages of development, and then set your goals and plan your strategies for reaching them.

CONTENTS

The evolution of the customer service concept. The roots of customer service: growth of mail order firms. Selling vs. marketing. Service vs. product. Defining customer service.

The service cycle. The customer profile. Essential customer needs. Strategies that provide customer service. Measuring the quality of customer service. Awards. Customer perceptions and expectations. Customer satisfaction. Handling customer complaints. The irate customer. The role of managers. Building customer relationships. The Deming method of quality control.

How do I begin? Job location, size of firm, type of
industry. Where do you find job leads? Making
your resume work for you. The interview makes a
difference. When the interview is over.

LIST OF FIGURES

CHAPTER 1

INTRODUCTION TO CUSTOMER SERVICE

To fully appreciate the full meaning of customer service, you need to gain an historical perspective on the different periods of time in American History that led to this concept. The first Americans and their descendants lived close to nature. Some led unstable lives as they hunted and gathered food for sustenance; others encountered harsh environments as they developed sophisticated farming methods and irrigation systems; and still others were skilled at handicrafts to the extent that some of their products could be used for storage and cooking.

The colonial economy was based primarily on agriculture and the production of raw materials. Pioneer life required an axe and a gun to clear the wilderness and set up farming. The raw products necessary for life were outside the door. Even though the work was hard and socializing was limited, the pioneer was his own master on his own land. In sum, the colonists were generalists who handled a variety of goods.

THE EVOLUTION OF THE
CUSTOMER SERVICE CONCEPT

Before industrialization, nearly 90 percent of the population lived on farms, most of them self-sufficient. People lived on what they could produce and purchased little that was made by others. To make items they needed in their homes, such as brooms for sweeping or hinges to hold doors in place, they improvised from materials they had available. Sometimes they exchanged their foodstuffs for services rendered by local artisans and mechanics.

Initially, the peddler who had products and wares to sell would carry his household merchandise on his back and go from farmhouse to farmhouse. Subsequently this selling method was replaced by horse and wagon, which also enabled the peddlers to carry a more varied inventory, including heavier merchandise such as pots and pans. With the development of the railroad system connecting major areas and with towns and small cities beginning to spring up, the peddlers began to open up shops, the forerunners of department stores. Gradually, agriculture too became market-oriented and developed along the lines of specialization; for example, rice was grown in the South, wheat in the Northeast, and tobacco in Virginia.

Even after the American Revolution, the United States was primarily an agricultural nation. Although general manufacturing did exist, the small farm family continued to make its own commodities for lack of funds and/or suppliers. Yet, even in this period, American entrepreneurs developed small mills for the manufacture of cotton goods, iron products, and other household items which paved the way for future industrial leadership. Until approximately 1850, manufacturing was primarily carried on in the home and shop by family labor or individual proprietors with apprentices, in contrast to the factory system as we know it where wages are received for work performed and where equipment is power-driven.

The Effects of the Industrial Revolution

The War of 1812 and the Civil War speeded up the Industrial Revolution. The factory system was introduced, big business began, and so did the early stages of the concentration of capital and the consolidation of businesses. Equipment was considered the major capital asset during the Industrial Age. People were considered to be only a means to profitability.

Agriculture continued to expand during this period. The population living on farms or in villages, largely supported by agriculture, was 30 million in 1860 and had expanded to 50 million by 1910. The number of farms tripled from two million to six million. Important scientific and technical changes occurred which revolutionized methods and increased production. Still, by the early 1900s, American agriculture was secondary to industry and was increasingly affected by the developing world capitalist society.

The tide of immigration during the 19th and early 20th centuries contributed to the country's growth both in agriculture and in the development of its natural resources. A 19th century writer observed that "Their coming is our benefit. They have built our railroads, cultivated our prairies, felled our forests, opened our mines, operated our mills, dug our gardens, and cooked, washed, and broke dishes in our kitchens." They influenced our cultural and political life.

All of these factors combine to give the United States a powerful capitalist economy. The number of quality products grew tremendously, as did consumers' demands for them. By the end of World War II, consumer demand for American products was so great that there was hardly any need to worry about improving a product or marketing it more successfully. The very existence of an American product sold itself.

Industry in the 1980s and 1990s began to face new challenges. Globalization of markets, pervasiveness of technology, growth patterns of industries such as electronics and computers, deregulation of industries such as airlines and banking, and shifts in channels of distribution (wholesalers, retailers, chains, discount outlets) led to a new customer service emphasis as a way to maintain a competitive edge. It is this service component that has become the significant factor in building a successful enterprise. Service has now become a primary product that needs to be managed and studied periodically.

We are living in a service economy, no longer like the industrial society of the 1940s. Approximately 90 percent of the American labor force will hold service jobs by the year 2000. As stated by Regis McKenna in ''Marketing Is Everything,''''The 1990s will belong to the customer.''

THE ROOTS OF CUSTOMER SERVICE: GROWTH OF MAIL ORDER FIRMS

The oldest mail order firms, Montgomery Ward and Co., Inc., (founded in 1872) and Sears, Roebuck and Co. (founded in 1891) fill customer orders from catalogs and circulars. Initially, they focused on farmers and people living in rural areas by supplying a variety of low-cost merchandise to them. With major population shifts in the early 1900s, the mail order firms began to establish retail stores across the country. These companies continued to fill orders for those customers who wished to order from catalogs as well as selling over-the-counter. A later innovation was the telephone ordering service where customers could call in their orders. Currently, many firms have a national toll-free telephone number for placing orders. In our modern economy, mail order firms play a significant role. Estimates indicate that between 15 and 20 percent of all general consumer merchandise is sold through the mail. These firms were probably the first that offered such services to their customers as full guarantees on merchandise, liberal adjustments, installment payments, and a generous return policy.

Sears' philosophy definitely has the customer in mind—buy for less, sell for less, but maintain quality. If you treat customers fairly, honestly, and generously, they will respond fairly, honestly, and generously. Most businesses have today adopted this philosophy.

SELLING VS. MARKETING

Selling is the function of producers of goods and services by which they generate income. Sellers may be individuals, small businesses, or large corporations. Marketing is the process of satisfying the needs of the customers. It includes creating, planning, executing, pricing, advertising, and distributing products.

Marketing is a team effort, according to Jeffrey P. Davidson in *The Marketing Sourcebook for Small Business:* "Your employees are customer or client contact points in your marketing effort." Employees must be knowledgeable about the entire organization so that they can answer questions typically asked by prospective customers. Ames and Hlavacek in *Managerial Marketing: The Ultimate Advantage* defined marketing as ". . .

a total business philosophy aimed at improving profit performance by identifying the needs of each key customer group and then designing and producing a product or service package that will enable the company to serve selected customer groups or segments more effectively than its competition."

This competition has grown tremendously in the past two decades. For example, twenty years ago IBM had only twenty competitors; today it has over five-thousand, including all companies that are in every aspect of the computer business. During the same time, many new customers have been gained—the great majority who now use or own a computer but did not use one in 1980. This led to a different marketing focus, one that was market-driven to serve the customer rather than sales-driven, centralizing on the product and assuming that price, features, and performance are the keys to sales. Regis McKenna in "Marketing is Everything" states that in a "time of exploding choice and unpredictable change . . . the solution is in marketing that finds a way to integrate the customer into the company, to create and sustain a relationship between the company and the customer." In effect, marketing is changing from manipulation of customer to customer involvement and the building of relationships.

SERVICE VS. PRODUCT

Service encompasses all strategies used to satisfy customers— the individuals who purchase, rent, or are involved in some aspect of the entire production and marketing process. Service is quality as well as the intangibles that lead to communicating information, creating a service reputation, and developing confidence in integrity of company. Frequently, customer service is difficult to control because of the large number of individuals involved, especially in "high contact" industries like the hotel business. Bro Uttal in "Companies That Serve You Best" states, "It's a day-in, day-out, ongoing, never-ending, unremitting, persevering, compassionate type of activity."

In the context of this book, the "product" is defined as a thing produced by labor and an asset that can be inventoried. The product may be equipment, software, or information. The book *Service America* says that a product can be distinguished from a commodity by the following characteristics:

- It is produced at the instant of delivery.
- It is delivered to the customer directly and cannot be centrally produced or kept in a warehouse.
- Samples cannot be provided nor demonstrations given.
- It is not a tangible item and is based on personal experience.
- It cannot be sold or passed on to another party.
- Improperly performed service cannot be recalled.
- Quality assurance must be performed before service is rendered.
- Human interaction occurs to some degree.
- Quality of service is subjective and is dependent on the receiver's expectations.

Quality control of a service differs from that of a product. The customer is the final judge of a service compared to a set of standards by which a product can be evaluated.

The above characteristics are not indicative of every service performed; however they reflect the special way buyer and seller conduct business.

DEFINING CUSTOMER SERVICE

It is not easy to define customer service because it is an aspect of every type of industry be it manufacturing, retailing, or service. Each type operates differently in trying to meet the goals of the business. For example, instead of providing service directly at the local store where an item such as a telephone answering unit was purchased, the equipment manufacturer may instead offer a limited warranty through a service center acting as an intermediary between the customer and the manufacturer. This particular procedure resolves customer complaints. More generally stated, all customer service activities aim to satisfy customers by providing information, a product, or a service. More sales, higher profits, and repeat business may be outcomes.

Ted Levitt in ''Marketing Success Through Differentiation— of Anything'' discusses his total product concept which enables business to focus on customer service that goes beyond what is normally expected. His model consists of four rings: generic, expected, augmented, and potential. The generic level consists of the fundamentals. The expected adds to the generic the now-traditional services customers have come to expect, such as timely delivery. The augmented adds benefits beyond customer expectations— such as a copy of each credit card purchase along with a fully itemized credit card statement. The potential adds services to attract and hold customers—services not typically found in most enterprises, such as a pianist who is hired to play music in the department store while shoppers browse and select merchandise they want to purchase.

Tom Peters in *Thriving on Chaos* suggests flip-flopping these four levels to reposition the product and create new markets by emphasizing the two outer rings: augmented and potential. He believes that ''service added'' is the edge needed to beat the competition. When other competitors begin to add the same services to the point that customers begin to expect them, then new ways need to be created to provide additional value to customers. Incorporating Levitt's philosophy, Uttal states, ''Customer service means all features, acts, and information that augment the customer's ability to realize the potential value of a core product or service.''

CHAPTER 2

THE NATURE OF CUSTOMER SERVICE

"The next decade will belong to those firms that break the cycle of failure. . . . it will belong to their customers and employees." (Schlesinger and Heskitt)

Customers are the most prized possession of a business. Their worth is more than the value of a single purchase; it is the long-term profit made from all purchases. The view of customer service is changing, and Americans are demanding more quality service than ever before. Tom Peters and Nancy Austin in *A Passion for Excellence* state that a business sells a quality service or product. The way to create and sustain superior performance is by exceptional care of customers via high-grade service and quality, along with constant innovation. These factors—service, quality, and innovation—are built on a foundation of "listening, trust, and respect for the dignity and the creative potential of each person in the organization."

THE SERVICE CYCLE

The service cycle, which begins at first point of contact between customer and organization, is defined by Karl Albrecht and Ron Zemke in *Service America* as ''a repeatable sequence of events in which various people try to meet the customer's needs and expectations at each point.'' For example, the cycle may begin with a telephone inquiry, a written request for merchandise, or a call to a travel agent to book an airline flight. Internally, employees in the organization may originate a cycle of service by dictating correspondence to the centralized dictation/transcription area, by setting up a meeting for the sales force, or by requesting that a call be placed to a particular job candidate for an interview.

Activities in the cycle that occur from initiation to fulfillment of customer's need can be identified. One individual must be made accountable for the events in the entire cycle. Through these cycles, the customer experiences the quality of service. The four factors below—identified by Karl Albrecht in *Service Within*—impact the quality of service experienced by the customer:

1. Complexity. A complex cycle may make it less likely that the customer will be happy.
2. Number of Players. The fewer people involved, the greater probability for customer satisfaction. People need to interact with one another and need to communicate information. The more players, the greater the risk of misunderstandings, misinformation, and lack of communication.
3. Transfers between Departments. Because each work group has different operating procedures and different views on rendering service, a lower rate of satisfaction may occur.
4. Customer Demands. The greater the demands in terms of knowledge and decision-making, the greater the possibility of something going wrong. The customer service representative must make every effort to understand the nature of customers' problems. Customers should not be placed in a

position where the responsibility is on them, for at this point customer service regresses to mediocrity.

Customer service cycles can spell failure as well as success. Instead of accepting cycles of failure, Leonard Schlesinger and James Heskett in ''Breaking the Cycle of Failure in Services'' state that service companies should learn from those companies who are successful. Some of the reasons for cycles of failure are poor managerial attitudes and belief that failure is beyond their control. They justify this by blaming people for not wanting to work, by stating that labor costs cannot be increased because it cannot be passed on to customers, and by believing that a high turnover rate is inevitable. Figure 1 reflects ''The Cycle of Failure'' and some of the leading causes: minimal selection effort, minimal training, employee boredom, payment of low wages, use of technology to control quality, and inability of employee to respond to customer problems.

An organization usually is a preferred employer if it has gained the reputation for good customer service. Schlesinger and Heskitt mention some techniques being used by companies to reverse the cycle of failure:

- A pay-for-performance plan to reward people for being productive;
- Job design and better task definition;
- Personal development and training activities;
- A ''Performance Plus'' program, such as that developed at Dayton's department store, which involves training, job redesign, and supervisory role modeling for sales associates. This program leads to superior customer service by sales consultants who go above the expected in fulfilling job responsibilities—such as sending thank you notes, informing customers of sales on new merchandise, and giving

discounts to long-standing customers in appreciation of patronage. These consultants are rewarded on a commission basis.
- A ''Partner-Manager'' program, like the one practiced at Au Bon Pain, where restaurant managers earn twice the industry

Figure 1   The Cycle of Failure

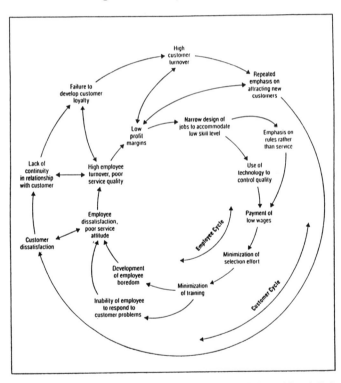

average—as much as $160,000 per year, five times more than managers at competing restaurants. Company and store management split profits over and above targets. Managers have the freedom to change procedures and staffing policies.
• Thanks to a considerable increase in customer service representatives' wages at Fidelity Bank of Philadelphia and the authorization given to service representatives to resolve all customer problems below $1,000, customer satisfaction in terms of willingness to recommend the bank to a friend jumped from 65 percent to 90 percent.

''The Cycle of Success'' in Figure 2 reflects strategies that perpetuated success, increased business, and led to higher profits. Some techniques included above average wages, extensive training, empowerment of frontline employees to control quality, intensified selection effort, emphasis on customer loyalty and retention, and broadened job designs.

To achieve cycles of success, frontline employees must operate consistently with a high level of concern for their customers; managers must be ready to step in and confront the problem issues. Successful organizations should not make excuses for poor results. Instead, they need to assume that an investment must be made to raise the organization's standards, communicate new expectations, implement new ways to achieve these expectations, and hire or train individuals with high standards.

THE CUSTOMER PROFILE

In today's economy, excellent customer service provides the competitive edge. Without it, an organization may fail. Customer services vary depending on target markets served, products

Figure 2   The Cycle of Success

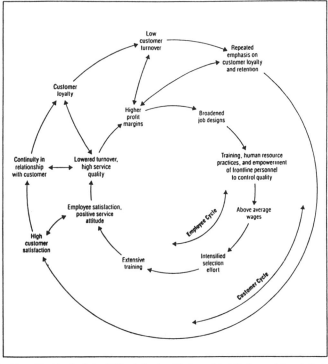

available for sale, location of customers, type of customer, competition in industry, trends in the marketplace, and gimmicks used to attract customers, such as free gifts. Before planning reorganizations and company strategies to attract and retain customers, a company must know who its customers are—then target this segment of the market. You can develop profiles for both customers as individuals and customers as organizations by asking a series of questions such as those listed below:

- What are your customers' names?
- Where do your customers live?
- What is the range of ages?
- Are your customers male, female, or both?
- What is their marital status?
- What is their educational level?
- In what types of occupations are they working?
- What is their economic level?
- How do your customers perceive your products and services? Which item is your best seller?
- What services do your customers value the most?
- Do your customers purchase your products consistently throughout the year, during special seasons and holidays, or are they transients?
- What is the total amount of purchases during the current year?
- What are the sales figures for purchases made during previous years?
- Is there a difference in sales of current year compared to the previous year?

Consumer and *customer* are terms frequently used to mean the same thing. "Consumers" actually are users of products; however, if they patronize a firm, then they become "customers" of that company. In effect, they are components of the whole customer system and all relationships must be considered as a single unit by a customer-oriented company, for one segment influences the other. Together with this concept must be appropriate systems, strategies, and products/services.

Customers, depending on type of industry or service organization, are known by different titles. For example, a broker calls his customers investors; bankers, depositors; airlines, passengers; lawyers, clients; retailers, customers; restaurateurs, diners; and manufacturers, dealers.

Frequently overlooked is the internal customer. Each department, division, or group has an important purpose in the organization. The customers are those individuals or departments that are affected by the work you do. Do you send statistical reports to anyone for decision-making? Does the administrative office service department transcribe and proofread executive correspondence? The recipients of the work you do are your customers. You should develop a profile of each of these customers, too. Find out if these individuals and departments are aware of all of the services you perform, and if you can be more helpful to them. Ask for an evaluation of the service they are presently receiving.

If an organization is the customer, a profile for the firm is also helpful. Your questions should relate to type of industry, size, location, and the cultural orientation of the organization—attitudes, values, preferences, and expectations.

ESSENTIAL CUSTOMER NEEDS

The basic critical needs of customers enumerated below are discussed by Jeffrey Davidson in *The Marketing Sourcebook for Small Business*.

Standards of Quality. Is the quality consistent? Does it greatly exceed standards and is the price at a level that customers can afford?

Services. Are services rendered sufficient and meeting customers' expectations?

Price. Is price the most important criterion used by customers? Do you offer more than your competitors, such as better quality and better service if the price is higher?

Communication. Do you make the time to meet with customers or to respond to their calls? Do you show that you care and want to meet their needs?

Conformance Standards. Can you meet standards of customers?

Innovation. Are you satisfied with the status quo, or do you constantly strive to improve your product, services, and reputation? Do you try to reduce costs through improved efficiency, passing on the savings to your customers?

Quality Measurement Program. Is the quality of your product or service consistently good?

Emergency Contingency Plan. Are such plans in place?

Nike, a retail store operation, follows the following basic guidelines that their customers would expect: convenient hours, courteous treatment, prompt service, handling complaints satisfactorily, varied selection of merchandise, pleasant environment, and bagging/wrapping of purchased goods.

STRATEGIES THAT PROVIDE CUSTOMER SERVICE

"Value in the eyes of the customer counts, not necessarily value in the eyes of the company's marketing or advertising people." (Albrecht and Zemke)

A strategy is an overall plan to make something work. "Successful strategies clearly segment customers by their service needs in order to concentrate on just a few, closely related segments," according to William Davidow and Bro Uttal in *Total Customer Service*. As indicated previously in this text, companies have to focus in on the customer, for you can't be all things to all people. You need to develop strategies that match your abilities to deliver service with the expectations of your target customers. If you are successful in providing superior service, this will distinguish you from your competitors and give you an edge over them.

When dealing with an individual customer, Marilyn and Tom Ross in *Big Marketing Ideas for Small Service Businesses* suggest the following strategies:

- Do not interrupt the customer who is complaining about something either in person or over the phone. Customers must be able to express themselves.
- Always invite a customer into your office or another private area for the sake of privacy.
- Ask open-ended question, using words such as "why," "what," "when," and "where."
- Listen to the customer.
- Permit the customer to state feelings before offering a solution.
- Use body language, such as an occasional nod, to indicate you understand and care about the customer.
- Be sympathetic and ask what the customer would like you to do.

Focus Groups. Another strategy would be to use focus groups to get reactions from your customers. Always relate your questions to an existing product and be sure your questions make sense to the customer. For example, a Swedish coffee firm noticed from its records that a previous purchaser and user of their coffee hadn't placed an order for some time. The two questions they asked that gave them the feedback they needed were: "Was there any reason you stopped purchasing their coffee?" Based on the response, which indicated that the customer was a small user of the product and had overpurchased, the next question was, "Would you use their service again when you run out of coffee?" The response was "Yes!"

Telemarketing. Use the telephone to stay in contact with your customers and clients.

Appearance and Body Language. Your appearance and body language reflect your genuineness about the product you are selling. Be knowledgeable about your product: be up-to-date with the latest changes so that you can be relaxed, thus putting your customer at ease. The use of the word "Yes" can reflect an understanding of the customer's problem, or it can show pleasure in having the product the customer needs.

Acknowledge a Customer's Presence. Greet customers, and if you are busy, just indicate you will serve them soon.

Listening. Listen to everything your customer does and does not say. This is the best way to understand a person's feelings and problems. This might make a difference in the way you resolve the situation.

Mirror the Customer. Through nonverbal communication, you can mirror the customer's feelings. If the customer shows enthusiasm, try to relate to the customer at the same level. If a person is reticent, don't push. One way of achieving this is to repeat words used by the customer. For example, the customer might say, "I am looking for a walking shoe with a soft innersole."

When bringing the shoe to the customer, the sales associate might say, "This shoe has a soft innersole."

Customer Journal. Maintain a personal customer journal about customers' preferences and needs. Thank you letters and holiday greeting cards remind customers about your service.

In Chapter 5 on "Industry Profiles," you will read more about specific strategies used by specific organizations.

MEASURING THE QUALITY OF CUSTOMER SERVICE

To maintain a high level of customer service, you must know how your customers feel about the current service you are providing so that you can determine if you are meeting their needs. Measuring the quality of customer service is a more difficult process than measuring the quality of a product. The former includes experiences and a person's behavior, while the latter is based on tangible items which have certain specifications and designated functions. Also, products can be controlled by setting standards; behaviors frequently depend on moods and feelings.

In *Managing Quality Customer Service,* William Martin refers to two dimensions which measure the quality of customer service: procedural and personal. Procedural refers to the process used to meet the needs of customers, such as the amount of time it takes to answer the telephone, the speed with which an order is filled, the communication of a problem to appropriate personnel for expeditious handling, and the feedback system on customer satisfaction. The personal dimensions relate to the human interaction of employee and customer: body language, tone of voice, appearance, sensitivity to customer's needs, and employee assistance.

A measurement system on the quality of customer service, according to Karl Albrecht in *Service Within,* should consist of the following components: a model, a feedback system, a method of analysis, and a reporting system of the results. Albrecht suggests the use of a customer report card for the quality model. Depending on your organizational objectives, the customers you serve, and the kinds of services you render, you may have to design one or more report cards. Include on this card factors you believe are valuable to your customers, as perceived by them. Examples of such factors are: attitudes of front-line employees; technical expertise of staff; friendliness of contact people; reliability of commitments, such as delivery time; ability to communicate in layman's terms; and availability of staff who can make quick decisions. Validation of all of the above factors should be made by your customers, selecting those that are really important.

The next step would be to get feedback from your customers. The use of surveys is frequently used for this purpose. Figure 3 is a copy of a Marriott Corporation customer survey. Similarly formatted guest questionnaires are used by hotels to determine the quality of housekeeping and room services. Surveys are also used to evaluate internal relationships of an organization, specifically designed for management, employees, or departments. The results of the surveys determine the effectiveness of the company's service policies, where the problems are, and whether there is a need to take corrective action. The system of measurement may have to be changed or modified. Surveys should be administered periodically for customer feedback, for they provide insight into customer satisfaction, including problem areas.

The next step is to analyze the data, using a system that scores each factor statistically. Statistical software packages are available for inexperienced personal computer users. The results of the analysis should then be distributed to all managers, key employees, and other related staff members. Be certain to include an explanation of the results and, if applicable, observed weaknesses of the system. This should be followed up by team meetings so that everyone becomes involved in providing quality customer service.

AWARDS

A change in corporate culture evolved with the growing emphasis on quality and a commitment to the customer rather than solely on profits. Initially quality processes were begun in manufacturing firms, such as Corning Glass, Xerox, and General Motors. Productivity was a concern of those employees who made the product, while quality related to customer satisfaction and was meaningful only if it met the needs and desires of customers. Gradually, quality programs entered the world of service industry organizations.

The Malcolm Baldrige Award

In recognition of exceptional quality programs, the United States Congress established in 1987 the Malcolm Baldrige National Quality Award—named after the first secretary of commerce in the Reagan administration. Motorola was the first recipient of this award. Some of the criteria established for award winners are listed on page 26.

Figure 3 How Well Did We Serve You?

We are always looking for ways to improve our food, service and restaurant atmosphere. Our commitment to you is prompt, friendly service and excellent food served in a clean and well maintained restaurant. Please take a moment and tell us how we did. Thank you.

Today's date is _____ .

Did you have . . .	Breakfast	Lunch
(circle one)	Dinner	Snack

How would you rate our service?

	Extremely Satisfied	Very Satisfied	Somewhat Satisfied	Slightly Satisfied	Not at all Satisfied
◆ Greeted and seated promptly	❏	❏	❏	❏	❏
◆ Friendliness	❏	❏	❏	❏	❏
◆ Speed	❏	❏	❏	❏	❏

How would you rate our food?

	Extremely Satisfied	Very Satisfied	Somewhat Satisfied	Slightly Satisfied	Not at all Satisfied
◆ Overall quality	❏	❏	❏	❏	❏
◆ Taste of food	❏	❏	❏	❏	❏

How would you rate your experience?

	Extremely Satisfied	Very Satisfied	Somewhat Satisfied	Slightly Satisfied	Not at all Satisfied
◆ Restaurant cleanliness	❏	❏	❏	❏	❏
◆ Value for your money	❏	❏	❏	❏	❏
◆ Overall dining experience	❏	❏	❏	❏	❏

How likely are you to return to a Bob's Big Boy Restaurant?

◆ I'll definitely return.   ❏
◆ I'll probably return.   ❏
◆ I may return.   ❏
◆ I probably won't return.   ❏
◆ I definitely won't return.   ❏

Additional Comments: _____

_____

_____

_____

_____

Restaurant Location: _____

1. involvement of top management
2. short- and long-term planning strategies
3. employee involvement in quality improvement programs
4. training for all employees of the company
5. measurement of customer needs and expectations and a plan for meeting these goals
6. a system for auditing internal quality management processes

Canada

Like the United States, Canada is also competing in a world of global markets; therefore, it, too, is targeting quality. The quality process at AVCO Financial Services of Canada was discussed by Patrick L. Townsend in *Commit to Quality.* The two elements of quality in AFS/Canada's "quality improvement process" are *Quality in Fact,* which is the performance of duties and responsibilities the right way, the first time, and on time; and *Quality in Perception,* which is a reflection of delivering the right product, satisfying customers' needs and meeting their expectations, and being courteous and respectful.

CUSTOMER PERCEPTIONS AND EXPECTATIONS

> "Turning service quality into a powerful competitive weapon requires continuous striving for service superiority—consistently performing above the adequate service level and capitalizing on opportunities for exceeding the desired service level." (Parasuraman, Berry, and Zeibaml)

In business, the only quality service that has merit is that which is perceived by the customer. The key is to know what customers expect and to respond to these expectations. Be aware, however, that these expectations can change after experience with the product or service. Customers begin to expect and take for granted those services that are normally provided. To give excellent service, you should anticipate the norm and then go above this level. Remember that service expectations in present society are greater than in previous years. Consumers are more sophisticated and more affluent; and with increasing competition, the choice of suppliers is greater. In addition, ever since the consumer movement that was begun in the sixties by Ralph Nader, consumer protection laws have evolved and agencies such as the Office of Consumer Affairs have been established by the government.

Research by Parasuraman *et al.,* on the nature of customers' service expectations and how companies can exceed these expectations, revealed the following conclusions:

- Customers want the basic services: namely, respectful treatment, explanations, technical competency, fair play, protection from catastrophes (major losses or accidents), prompt service, honesty, upholding commitments, speed of response, flexibility, availability of products and parts, and prompt refunds.
- The service process is the key to providing more than the basics customers expect. Actions that demonstrate understanding of the customer's needs and that usually go beyond the usual company commitments concern responsiveness (providing prompt service), assurance (demonstration of trustworthiness), and empathy (concern for customer).
- Customer service expectations have two levels: the desired and the adequate (minimum performance level expected by customers). Adequate service levels may change depending on particular circumstances, such as a breakdown in a computer system. Managers need to understand these changeable

levels of customer expectations and must exceed both service levels for competitive advantage.

- Customers want relationships and want the person-to-person contact. They want to deal with the same representative and want to feel that they will be contacted by the representative when it is beneficial for them to receive certain information and advice.

"Genuine customer relationships are built on the foundation of fairness, sincere efforts to understand and help the customer, and ongoing personalized communications . . ."

CUSTOMER SATISFACTION

John Goodman of Tarp Institute, Washington, D.C., in his "National Quality Day" speech, defined customer satisfaction as "the state in which customer needs, wants, and expectations are met or exceeded, resulting in repurchase and continued loyalty." A satisfied customer has a value greater than money can buy. Tarp designed and implemented customer satisfaction improvement strategies used by major companies throughout the world. Tarp Institute's formula for achieving customer satisfaction, illustrated in "Making Customer Satisfaction a Profit Center," follows:

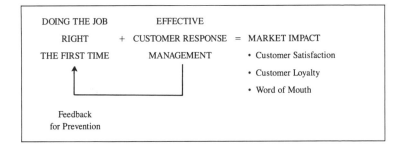

```
DOING THE JOB          EFFECTIVE
    RIGHT        +  CUSTOMER RESPONSE  =  MARKET IMPACT
THE FIRST TIME        MANAGEMENT          • Customer Satisfaction
                                          • Customer Loyalty
                                          • Word of Mouth


   Feedback
 for Prevention
```

Doing the Job Right the First Time is the most important determinant of customer satisfaction. As indicated previously in this book, organizations that achieve customer satisfaction generally are managed and staffed by a group of highly motivated employees who are committed to their customers. The efforts of each and every one of these individuals lead to customer satisfaction.

No matter how successful a company is, problems do occur that are disruptive to both company and customer. Therefore, the company needs to have an effective system to handle these problems and questions as they develop. TARP refers to this component of the customer satisfaction formula as *Effective Customer Response Management*. These responses are the feedback used to identify and correct customer problems, which then leads to customer satisfaction, loyalty, and positive word-of-mouth statements about continuing to do business with the company.

An approach on building partnerships that achieves customer satisfaction is discussed by Sobel and Hines in "Cray's New Focus on Customers." They believe "an integrated system of policies, programs and initiatives that focuses on customer needs" includes seven key components:

1. *Company Philosophy*—definition of customer service and expected behaviors of employees;
2. *Assessment*—determination of current level of customer satisfaction; to learn of problem areas, to realize customer's investment to company, to gather information to use in marketing, planning, and operations;
3. *Practices*—a clarification of roles and responsibilities of employees in various departments;
4. *Human Resource Management*—a new focus on new hires, performance expectations, training, and rewards;

5. *Training*—a means of expanding employees' knowledge, skills, and attitudes to improve customer service;
6. *Communication*—to provide employees and customers with information and to determine the expectations of customers;
7. *Action*—to implement all of the plans listed above to achieve customer satisfaction.

At Cray Research, Inc., "In the eyes of the customer, the employee is the organization. . . ." Several key factors that contribute to the maintenance of a high level of customer satisfaction are the following: honesty with customers, visibility and accessibility, careful listening and response to customer, demonstration of ability to perform, and use of company and customer resources effectively.

HANDLING CUSTOMER COMPLAINTS

According to an expert, "most companies spend 95 percent of their resources handling complaints and less than 5 percent analyzing them." This shows a misallocation of resources because it is more important to determine the cause first, so that preventative measures can be taken to retain customers by avoiding the recurrence of similar problems. A look at some statistics on customer problem experiences reveals interesting customer behavior patterns. According to The National Consumer Survey (NCS), sponsored by the United States Office of Consumer Affairs, approximately one-third of the households in the interview experienced at least one consumer problem during the year preceding the survey. This resulted in financial losses and/or lost time at work. In another research study, one out of four purchases resulted in some type of problem; still another revealed that more than 70 percent of the respondents experienced problems with grocery products.

How do these unhappy customers react when they have a problem? Research revealed that more than 70 percent of the respondents who had problems with products or services did not complain. Of those who do complain, TARP found that approximately 45 percent complain to front-line sales representatives or to the retailer, and 5 percent complain to management. Organizations should examine the reasons that customers do not complain because they are the ones who are least loyal to the company. The three principal reasons are: it isn't worth their time and effort; no one really cares or will do anything about the problem; and they don't know how or where to make the complaint.

Customer complaints that are handled properly pay off handsomely to the company for three basic reasons, according to Michael LeBoeuf in *How to Win Customers and Keep Them For Life:*

1. Complaints highlight areas that need improvement and where to take action to correct a problem.
2. Complaints give the company a second chance to provide service and satisfaction to complainants so that they can retain them as satisfied customers.
3. Complaints are an opportunity to strengthen customer loyalty. Boeuf states that 95 percent of the customers will buy again if complaints are resolved immediately and 70 percent will remain loyal if the problem is settled in their favor.

Figure 4 below reflects the percentage of loyal customers who had minor complaints or major complaints, and shows why it is in the best interests of a company to solicit and handle complaints

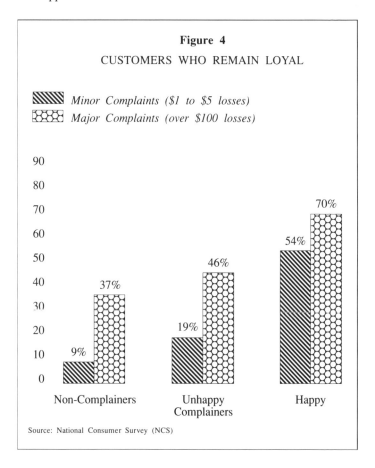

Figure 4

CUSTOMERS WHO REMAIN LOYAL

▨▨▨ *Minor Complaints ($1 to $5 losses)*
⬡⬡⬡ *Major Complaints (over $100 losses)*

Source: National Consumer Survey (NCS)

quickly and satisfactorily. Think in terms of long-range goals, too. Surely keeping a customer happy is worth more than a small loss of money—especially when considered in terms of revenue brought in by this customer. It gives corporations a powerful marketing edge over their competition.

An important factor to keep in mind is that the American consumer is heavily influenced by word-of-mouth statements, both positive and negative, according to a study conducted by TARP for the Corporate Consumer Affairs Department of The Coca-Cola Company. Complainants tell twice as many people as do satisfied customers. This does have a strong impact on sales.

Guidelines for Handling Complaints

The quality of customer service depends on the procedures and behaviors used to manage complaints as well as processes used in normal situations. Every employee needs to understand both the impact of complaints on business and the ways in which they can be resolved satisfactorily as perceived by the customer. Below are some suggestions for handling complaints:

- Receive complaints as opportunities to improve designs or procedures. Analyze them to find out root cause.
- Listen carefully to customers and attempt to resolve problem quickly.
- Show concern in your behavior and remarks.
- Document and log in complaints. Paraphrase the complaint to verify accuracy.
- Determine what the customer desires and propose a solution. If customer dissatisfaction is apparent, ask for an alternative and try to settle it promptly.
- Be certain the customer is satisfied before he or she leaves the store or gets off the telephone.
- Make follow-up calls to make certain the customer is satisfied.
- Never argue with a customer.
- Set measurable goals for handling complaints.

THE IRATE CUSTOMER

Some situations are more difficult to handle than others, particularly when you have an irate customer. You, the employee, must recognize that the customer has a problem. The customer is *not* the problem. Generally, the difficulty occurs when the customer's expectations are not met. To resolve a situation, quick and decisive action needs to be taken that will satisfy the customer. As stated previously under the guidelines for handling complaints, never argue with a customer—even if you know you are right. Try to diffuse the customer's anger by being friendly, agreeing when appropriate, and showing a concerned attitude. You should focus on the problem, be empathetic and helpful, listen to customer's complaint, indicate what you can do, and respond immediately by assuming responsibility for resolving it to the customer's satisfaction. Thank the customer for bringing the matter to your attention and offer additional assistance.

Training for both managers and other employees does make a difference in the performance of their duties, mainly to provide superior service to customers and to handle complaints effectively. This will be discussed further in Chapter 6.

THE ROLE OF MANAGERS

The role of management in a service-driven organization "is to enhance the culture, set expectations of quality, provide a motivating climate, furnish the necessary resources, help solve problems, remove obstacles, and make sure high-quality job performance pays off." (Albrecht and Zemke)

A service-driven organization is a "top-down" concern. The management must be committed to a service goal, and this customer service vision must be communicated to the entire organization. Management must be a model for the entire staff. Bro Uttal believes every manager and employee has to get involved in the company in which they are employed if it is to excel in customer service. Succinctly stately, each one has "to get the service religion." An environment has to be developed in which the entire organization is responsive to the needs of both internal and external customers.

What are some of the qualities of a good manager? Most important, as stated previously, managers need to believe in a customer service philosophy and in communicating this with their staff. Service is not only what is done for the customer but the total experience of the customer.

Managers cannot insulate themselves from problems as they arise and expect customer service departments to be the sole arbiters. They, too, need to deal with the situations at every service level. Managers need to develop effective service strategies, listen to their employees, motivate their subordinates to provide the best service possible to the customers, praise employees to show appreciation, inspire employees by acting as a role model, involve employees in goal setting and innovative procedures, and hire individuals with personalities that can develop to a customer orientation.

Managers must remember that the employees should share the company's customer service vision, for they are the individuals who will make it happen. Satisfied employees will produce satisfied customers. A study of employees conducted by the University of Delaware, as reported in the October 1991 issue of *Working Woman,* found that workers who feel "genuinely valued" will give back more in both time and creativity. They are generally committed to working harder and contributing innovative ideas to increase productivity and profits.

Appropriate to the above discussion, Frederick Herzberg, a behavioral scientist, created a theory of motivation based on two sets of job factors: motivation factors, which relate to job content and can increase job satisfaction, and hygiene factors, which pertain to the job environment and do not increase job satisfaction. The motivation factors are particularly important in service-driven organizations; they have no limit. The more you motivate, the greater the number of satisfied employees. Managers need to provide employees with the chance to be successful, to perform challenging work, to be responsible for one's performance, to be recognized for achievement, and to have opportunities for advancement and growth. These satisfiers clearly relate to the top two levels of Abraham Maslow's hierarchy of needs: esteem needs and self-actualization needs. A supportive statement by authors William Wagel and Hermine Zagat Levine in *HR '90: Challenges and Opportunities* states: ''Autocratic managers need to change to a participative style of management.'' The traditional form of hierarchal management must give way to employee involvement and participation. Another supportive remark was made by Martin John Yate in *To Serve Customers Serve Employees.''* ''It is employees—not management—who make the ultimate difference.'' Employees and management need to be committed to the same vision.

BUILDING CUSTOMER RELATIONSHIPS

Genuine customer relationships are built on the foundation of fairness, sincere efforts to understand and help the customer, and ongoing, personalized communications—at-

tributes of service most demonstrable during delivery.
(Parasuraman, Berry, and Zeitbaml)

A product by itself cannot build a relationship. A similar one frequently can be supplied by a competitor. Customers want personalized relationships with providers who are loyal and who understand their business or personal requirements. They want to be in contact with the same employee, a representative who understands their needs, recognizes them as regular customers, and cares about satisfying them. Relationships don't just happen; you need to cultivate them. For example, if a problem arises where you may not be able to fulfill an order on schedule, contact the customer, explain the circumstances, and outline your plan to provide service. This procedure shows honesty, involves the customer, and develops a trusting relationship. These relationships are most important in exceeding customer expectations. The editor of the 1991 edition of Harvard Business Review cites five challenges companies can meet to get closer to their customers:

1. *Understanding the Customer.* All relationships are important, each influencing the others. All customers need to be part of the process.
2. *Turning Customers into Members.* Membership groups of users serve as test sites and share ideas. When word processors were first introduced, vendors held training sessions and offered in-house assistance. However, with the spread of computers, vendor manuals replaced company service. This resulted in the growth of computer clubs where networks were formed for problem-solving. Companies recognized the advantages of such groups and established other membership groups such as the Lego Builders Club and hot lines.

3. *Making Customers Real to All Employees*. Some companies have programs to test innovations in which employees take the role of the customer. Others invite customers to see plant operations.
4. *Using Customer Data to Benefit Customers*. Gathering, analyzing, and using data to meet the specific needs of customers is a relatively easy process with the use of a computer and database program.
5. *Keeping Promises by Championing Change*. Only company promises that can be kept are positive factors. Those that aren't upheld are dangerous, frequently a result of a needed change in company operations and structure which might be costly.

Maintaining a relationship can be encouraged through a variety of activities such as calling on customers, telephoning to say hello and to receive feedback, sending a note or card for holidays, taking a customer out to lunch, being friendly and sincere, and taking time out to just talk.

THE DEMING METHOD OF QUALITY CONTROL

No book on customer service would be complete without reference to Dr. W. Edwards Deming's philosophy of quality control. To him, quality is meaningful only in terms of the customer and his or her needs. The process begins with a commitment from top management and needs to filter down to employees, suppliers, and consumers. Deming believes that you must study the consumer, his likes and dislikes, and then create a product that brings repeat customers. His impact on management methods began in 1950 when he went on a mission to Japan to teach them how they could join the leading industrial nations of the world by improving quality. Quality, Deming believes, lowers costs and increases productivity. His success was apparent when in 1951 the Japanese established the Deming Prize to be awarded to companies that best implement Deming's theories.

American industry apparently wasn't ready to accept Deming's ideas until Japanese products, such as automobiles, steel, and electronic equipment began penetrating our markets. One of his strongest supporters in America turned out to be Donald Petersen, a former chairman and chief executive officer of Ford Motor Company. The basic premise of Deming's method is that companies are in business to provide jobs; profits subsidize a business and provide workers with a livelihood so that they can work to create products that enhance the quality of life. Concomitantly, employees need to be an integral part of the system, need to participate in decision-making, and need to have a sense of pride in their own work.

The Deming method involves everyone and every aspect of the company—management, employees, equipment, supplies, and environment. Deming based his method on Fourteen Points which encompass a philosophy of management in conjunction with statistical procedures. The first, to "create constancy of purpose for the improvement of product and service" encompasses his entire philosophy of quality control. In effect, it means that you need to design and redesign processes that will work; relationships with suppliers need to be cultivated so that quality is maintained. The second through the fourteenth points concern management and labor. They focus mainly on the philosophy of workmanship and service, improvement of process rather than inspection, quality supplies and workmanship, training programs, leadership, teamwork, quotas, and barriers that affect performance.

To *build the skills and attitudes* necessary for a thriving customer-service oriented organization, a training program is critical. Unlike prior decades when capital investments were made primarily for plant and equipment, budgets now allocate a substantial amount of money for employee training. For further discussion, read Chapter 6.

CHAPTER 3

THE OPPORTUNITIES

The major factors that have had an impact on occupations are global markets, the shift from a goods-producing to a service-producing economy, modifications in consumer preferences, and changes in business organizations and management. Customer service is one of the developing fields of employment.

A broad range of job opportunities exists in both small firms and large corporations as well as in all types of industries and the professions: retail, manufacturing, banking, insurance, restaurant, transportation, public utilities, health care, travel agencies, advertising, publishing, and many more. These jobs range from entry-level positions, such as over-the-counter clerk in a retail establishment, to professional positions in financial and medical organizations. Position titles vary depending on the type of firm and department in which you are employed. Similarly, there is a wide diversity of position responsibilities and duties. Look at the "Help Wanted" ads which appear in any Sunday newspaper and you will clearly see the range of career opportunities that are available. There is, however, one common factor in each of these jobs—the demand to provide customer service.

In this chapter, you will learn about the different types of customer service careers you can pursue, the requirements of the job, and the salaries paid at various levels of employment.

A 1989 Customer Service Compensation Study sponsored by International Customer Service Association (ICSA) gathered data about growth, functions performed, educational requirements, and salaries in service professions. The results indicated below are based on responses from 628 participating ICSA firms.

CUSTOMER SERVICE (CS) TITLES AND POSITION DESCRIPTIONS

As you read the following job descriptions, think about the different types of industries and departments in which these positions exist. Also, note that the designation "customer service" is not a part of every position title, even though the employee is performing such functions.

CS Clerk. Performs routine filing, clerical, typing, and similar functions.

Order Entry Clerk. Audits and batches all incoming order entry documentation for computer output or, with online systems, enters orders on CRT terminal, and maintains entry reports.

CS Representative. Receives and processes all incoming orders and prepares appropriate forms for invoices; responds to customers on product availability, delivery, complaints, and returns; and initiates credit checks.

Senior CS Representative or *Assistant CS Supervisor.* Acts as a team leader, account executive, or working supervisor. Takes orders; handles routine inquiries, complaints, claims, credits, and refunds below a certain dollar amount. Has extensive knowledge of account requirements, resolves customer problems by cutting through red tape, handles exceptions and special problems.

Order Processing Manager/Supervisor. Has equivalent rank to Assistant Manager of Customer Service or CS Supervisor. Receives orders; edits and reviews orders; performs credit checks; maintains records dealing with order processing system (order status, inventory, backorders); trains, motivates, and supervises order entry clerks and support personnel; controls security of customer records and computer databanks; supervises entry of new data and product descriptions; processes orders for supplies, maintains equipment, and handles service contracts.

Assistant Manager of CS or CS Supervisor. Processes orders, claims, and returns above a certain dollar limit and warranty administration; acts as liaison with sales, credit, inventory control, warehousing, shipping, traffic, data processing, and the customer; serves as operating head of department in absence of CS Manager; performs special functions such as customer research and development of CS manual.

CS Manager. Trains personnel, monitors performance, introduces efficient procedures, writes and/or updates customer service manuals, maintains customer files, recommends changes, handles order processing, and receives claims, returns, and inquiries on billing, adjustments, and products.

The position description in the *1989 Management Salary Survey* adds that the CS manager is responsible for the customer service department, establishes policy and guidelines for responding to service requests and service complaints, provides procedures for making decisions on service charges and writing off charges within a company's allowable limits, and keeps operating managers informed of product service trends.

CS Director. Directs the operational and administrative functions of the customer service department(s); participates in long-range planning, assigns goals and objectives to the CS manager(s), provides direction, implements policies, plans budgets, hires, and sets standards.

Other job categories that were not specifically indicated in the ICSA survey but which you ought to be aware of as you search for a career are discussed below.

Customer Order Recording Specialist. Works in a telemarketing center where requests are received, inventories are checked, items ordered, purchases are confirmed, and purchase orders are sent to the billing and shipping departments

Computer Assisted Sales Representative. Helps customers select computers with graphics capabilities.

Information Retrieval and Reproduction Clerk. Develops list of "key words" that are indexed for customer information and document retrieval. Works in all types of offices where electronic filing systems are kept.

Loan and Credit Clerk and Credit Authorizer. Reviews credit history and rating of applicant and obtains information needed to determine creditworthiness. These clerks are involved in the processing or closing of a loan. Processing clerks research the background information by contacting credit bureaus and reporting agencies for the applicant's records and verifies all personal and financial information supplied. Clerks involved in closing loans verify documents by reviewing loan file and insure completeness of document.

Credit Authorizers review customer's credit records and payment history and make final decision on approval of customer's credit card purchase.

Other occupations related to credit clerks and authorizers are customer complaint clerks, probate clerks, collection clerks, claim examiners, and claim adjusters.

A new career path is *customer administrator* or *systems administrator.* The responsibilities of this person include overseeing systems and keeping lists up to date.

CUSTOMER SERVICE FUNCTIONS

The ICSA study found that at least 75 percent of the respondents handled general inquiries, order status inquiries, phone order processing, price and availability of product, and acted as liaison with other departments. Figure 5 below shows by rank order the customer service functions performed by respondents:

In addition to the above functions performed by customer service representatives, those employees who are in the computer industry may frequently diagnose and solve problems over the telephone when the customer calls for help, may assign workers to correct specific problems, and may perform the work expected of a work-order control clerk. In the 1991 revised edition of *The Dictionary of Occupational Titles,* under the category of Occupations in Computer Systems User Support, the alternate titles for the position of user support analyst include customer service representative, end-user consultant, help desk representative, information center specialist, and office automation analyst. These jobs are "concerned with investigating, resolving, and explaining computer-related problems to users of computer systems."

QUALIFICATIONS FOR CUSTOMER
SERVICE POSITIONS

You read in the first two chapters that the decade of the 1990s and beyond will belong to the customer. A company product in and of itself will probably no longer retain customer loyalty; a high level of customer service will. In fact, customer service duties are becoming an important part of most positions.

Figure 5

CUSTOMER SERVICE FUNCTIONS PERFORMED
(N638)

Function	% of Companies
Inquiries	92
Order Status Inquiries	83
Liaison with Other Departments	78
Phone Order Processing	76
Price/Availability	75
Returns/Claims Processing	69
Mail Order Processing	64
Field Sales Support	56
Sales Literature Request	54
Inside Rep Training	52
Inside Rep Supervision	41
Direct Inside Selling	21
Sales Lead Qualification	19
Other Inside Supervisory	18
Credit and Collection	17
Miscellaneous	17

SOURCE: *1989 Compensation Study,* ICSA

Employees in these positions need the right combination of skills, knowledge, behavioral attitudes, and personality. The jobs generally require a knowledge of company's service policies and procedures; good oral and written communications; computational skills; ability to search for and gather information; selling skills; decision-making and problem-solving skills; knowledge about office technology such as voice mail and the personal computer; human relations skills; and personal qualities that include a pleasant speaking voice, patience, sincerity, tact, a courteous manner, and a neat appearance. In ''This Way to Success'' in *The Office Professional* (August, 1991), to be a top *quality* employee, you need to:

1. Make a commitment to yourself to strive for continuous personal and professional growth. Acquire new skills, become knowledgeable about the company for which you work, be sensitive to people, be committed to team work and its goals.
2. Design your own improvement plan.
3. Use your knowledge on the job to add value to the company for which you work.

SALARIES

As you examine salary surveys when considering a career decision, analyze them in terms of geographic location of the company, ease of access, availability of applicants, fringe benefits, working environment, nature of the job, and promotional opportunities. Equally important to recognize is that it wasn't until 1987 when many service firms began to develop formal customer service operations, which might indicate that with growth a career ladder for this profession will gradually evolve.

Since 1987, according to the ICSA study, salaries for most customer service professionals have increased between 5 percent and 10 percent. Figure 6 below shows the average salary in several regions of the U. S. and Canada for each of the positions described in the ICSA 1989 Customer Service Compensation Study. As you examine these salaries, you will notice that the average salary in the United States is highest in the Northeast for CS clerk; in the South Central, for CS representative, senior CS representative, assistant CS manager, and CS director; in the Mountain/Pacific area, for entry clerk and CS manager. The figures do not reflect a consistent pattern in each area. Similarly, Canada, compared to the United States, only shows higher average salaries for two positions, CS clerk and entry clerk.

Figure 6

AVERAGE ANNUAL SALARY BY SELECTED REGIONS

Job Classification	Area 1	Area 2	Area 3	Area 4	Canada
CS Director	$55,196	$54,224	$57,403	$52,635	$50,400
CS Manager	40,551	40,935	39,657	41,033	37,224
Asst. CS Manager	30,507	30,217	31,577	31,146	28,646
Order Proc. Manager	30,073	28,698	29,665	29,741	27,711
Senior CS Representative	24,985	24,697	26,475	23,556	24,787
CS Representative	20,684	20,343	22,068	22,051	20,137
Entry Clerk	17,243	16,842	15,244	17,903	18,614
CS Clerk	15,750	16,336	14,956	16,029	16,392

Legend: Area 1 – All Regions
          Area 2 – Northeast (ME, NH, MA, RI, CT, NJ, NY, PA, MD, WV, VT, DE)
          Area 3 – South Central (TX, OK, LA, AK, MS, KY, TN, AL)
          Area 4 – Mountain Pacific (WA, OR, CA, NV, ID, MT, WY, UT, AZ, NM, CO, HI, AK)

A look at the salary ranges in Figure 7 will give you some insight into the beginning and top payment received for these positions. You will notice that the increment ranges from approximately $7,000 to $7,400, except for the South Central geographical area, which is $6,300.

Figure 7

ANNUAL SALARY RANGES BY SELECTED REGIONS

Job Classification	Area 1	Area 2	Area 3	Area 4	Canada
CS Director					
Starting	$44,577	$43,758	$45,279	$42,205	$44,270
Top	67,198	64,398	71,716	65,954	58,743
CS Manager					
Starting	32,812	32,771	32,854	33,698	31,551
Top	48,474	48,842	47,207	48,242	44,194
Asst. CS Manager					
Starting	24,957	25,004	26,233	25,525	25,223
Top	36,656	36,543	38,114	36,499	34,262
Order Proc. Manager					
Starting	23,951	23,206	22,972	24,258	23,412
Top	35,705	34,700	33,117	34,354	32,777
Senior CS Rep.					
Starting	20,546	20,627	21,798	20,322	20,924
Top	29,079	29,489	30,220	27,265	28,601
CS Representative					
Starting	17,039	16,877	18,461	16,720	16,801
Top	24,657	24,285	24,814	23,694	24,169
Entry Clerk					
Starting	14,635	14,330	13,495	14,950	16,188
Top	20,239	19,502	17,473	20,961	21,100
CS Clerk					
Starting	13,310	13,852	13,229	13,396	14,418
Top	18,424	18,866	16,816	18,245	19,480

Legend: Area 1 – All Regions
Area 2 – Northeast (ME, NH, MA, RI, CT, NJ, NY, PA, MD, WV, VT, DE)
Area 3 – South Central (TX, OK, LA, AK, MS, KY, TN, AL)
Area 4 – Mountain Pacific (WA, OR, CA, NV, ID, MT, WY, UT, AZ, NM, CO, HI, AK)

Other salary data used by compensation managers and company recruiters to determine salaries for various levels of employees reveal that the U.S. average weekly salary for customer service representatives is approximately the same for personnel clerks but higher than for purchasing clerks, credit and collection clerks, senior general clerks, and switchboard operators. (See Figure 8.) For managerial positions, salaries appear to be higher in the manufacturing/processing/construction industries than in the other types of businesses. (See Figure 9.)

The findings of the ICSA study also indicated that employees with college degrees will earn more money than a high school graduate. At entry level, the increase ranges from approximately $3,000 to well over $13,328.

You should be aware of a fairly new concept that is evolving whereby employees can receive salary increments for learning new skills or adding to their knowledge base. This idea is known as "pay-for-knowledge system," "pay for service," "pay-for-learning," or "skill-based pay." Employees have to leave their

Figure 8

AVERAGE WEEKLY SALARY
FOR SELECTED OFFICE PERSONNEL
Total United States

Position Title	*Weekly Salary*
Customer Service Representative	$348
Personnel Clerk	347
Purchasing Clerk	342
Senior General Clerk	333
Credit and Collection Clerk	327
Switchboard Operator	291

SOURCE: 1989 Office Salaries Report, Administrative Management Society

Figure 9

AVERAGE ANNUAL SALARIES
FOR SELECTED MANAGERIAL POSITIONS
by Type of Business

(annual salaries in thousands)

Position Title	Type 1	Type 2	Type 3
Customer Service Manager	36.6	32.5	32.1
Credit and Collection Manager	37.5	31.3	32.2
Purchasing Manager	42.8	32.9	33.7
Personnel Manager	43.6	46.9	38.7
Marketing Manager	55.4	51.9	46.2

Source: 1989 Office Salaries Report, Administrative Management Society, 1989, p. 10.

LEGEND
Type 1– Manufacturing/Processing/Construction
Type 2 – Banking/Finance/Insurance
Type 3 – Service (Business, Employment, Entertainment, etc.)

workstations less frequently to search for answers; employers find productivity increases, as does customer satisfaction. The components of one insurance company's program are base pay linked to the number of services an employee provides, and performance incentives linked to customer satisfaction and cost of doing business. The employees in this company are divided into teams and subteams of individuals who provide on-the-job training in new service skills and who also attend formal classroom training courses.

FRINGE BENEFITS

Fringe benefits have substantial value in terms of compensation and should be considered when evaluating a salary for a designated position. Plans vary from company to company and particularly when the economy is in a recession. In the past, where some firms covered hospitalization and health insurance completely, they may now require employees to contribute a portion of it. Other benefits may include life insurance, pension plans, and vacations. In some companies, these benefits, are now being replaced by "cafeteria plans," a flexible arrangement from which an employee selects from a menu of choices, including health and dental insurance, life insurance, prescription drug plan, childcare coverage, and elder care provisions. If you have such a choice, weigh all of the options when making a selection and cover yourself if a medical emergency arises, particularly in view of the rising costs of health care.

CHAPTER 4

THE NEED FOR CUSTOMER SERVICE PERSONNEL

To fully understand why the demand for specific types of personnel fluctuates, you should be aware of the changing character of the labor market and work force that has occurred over the last decade. An area that has been receiving increasing emphasis in the past few years is customer service, the focus of this book. You will read more about labor market statistics and the nature of the labor force in the sections that follow.

LABOR MARKET STATISTICS

The labor market of the 1990s is changing from that of the previous decades. A shift is occurring in employment from goods-producing to service-producing industries. Within this sector, service is both the largest and fastest growing industry. Bureau of Labor Statistics data indicate that services provided for 34.5 million jobs in 1988 and that by the year 2000 this figure will increase to 44.2 million, a 28 percent increase. Half of all new jobs will be in services, in both small firms and large corporations as well as in all types of industries and in government. Those with the largest employment growth rate will be the health services and business services, a projected growth from 8.2 to 11.3 million in health services and from 5.6 million to 8.3 million in business services by the year 2000. In the latter group, personnel supply services, which includes temporary help agencies, will account for the largest number of new jobs.

Another interesting phenomenon is the marked restructuring in the way America does business. There has been a resurgence of entrepreneurship which is gaining a strong foothold in American industry. Entrepreneurs are individuals who organize and operate their own business. They assume full responsibility for the firm and make all of their own decisions: organization, location, product, price, and hours.

Marketing, a field involved in bringing products to market and influencing consumers to buy them, offers many opportunities for customer service employment. As large a field as it is, the demand for marketing, advertising, and public relations services is expected to grow because of increased global competition. Also, the need to supply goods and services to an increasing population will create opportunities for employment in both wholesale and retail firms. To understand the vastness of this field, stop and think about the many ways in which sales are solicited, such as through flyers, advertisements, samples, telephone solicitations, catalogs, discount coupons, radio announcements, television programs, and billboards. Opportunities exist throughout the country in a diversity of firms that include manufacturers, advertising agencies, consulting firms, retailers, securities and financial firms, and product testing laboratories.

The process of marketing begins before a product exists or reaches the consumer. The financial advisability of producing a product needs to be researched; distribution channels that might include wholesale, retail, and direct marketing need to be determined; a sales force needs to be trained; and a promotion strategy needs to be developed. Even after sales are consummated, marketing doesn't stop. A company must be ready to respond to customers' inquiries and to resolve problems. Some titles of individuals who are involved in the marketing process are field representatives, or interviewers; research analysts; field coordinator; account representatives or assistant account executives; marketing communications specialists; public relations director; field sales representatives; and information clerk.

Figure 10, from the Bureau of Labor Statistics, shows 1986 employment figures in marketing occupations and the projection for the year 2000. The largest growth rate, a 56 percent increase, is anticipated for service sales representatives, followed by interview clerks, 45 percent.

The 1990–1991 American Almanac of Jobs and Salaries indicates that while the population was growing by almost 50 percent between 1950 and 1989, the labor force increased by 140 percent. The most startling change was in the growth of the number of women entering the labor force, from 30 percent of the total work force in 1950 to over 45 percent in 1989. By the turn of this century, 81 percent of the women in the U.S. will be working and will account for 47 percent of the nation's labor force.

Changes in Employment. With the shift from goods-producing industries to service-producing industries, it is obvious that by the year 2000 nearly four out of five jobs will be in industries that provide service. Several factors have led to this change: consumer preferences and greater awareness, technological growth, regulatory changes, and differences in the way in which business is organized and managed. In the retail trade alone, by the year 2005, 5.1 million additional jobs are projected, compared to state and local governments with 3.2 million and finance, insur-

Figure 10

PROJECTED EMPLOYMENT IN MARKETING OCCUPATIONS,
1986–2000

Title	1986 Employment (thousands)	2000 Employment (thousands)	% Change 1986–2000
Economists and market research analysts	37	50	34
Insurance sales workers	463	565	22
Interview clerks	104	150	45
Manufacturers' sales workers	543	561	3
Marketing, advertising, and public relations managers	323	427	32
Order clerks	271	277	2
Order fillers	195	208	7
Public relations specialists	87	122	40
Retail sales workers	4,266	5,611	32
Service sales reps	419	656	56

ance, and real estate with 1.4 million. Overall, employment will probably increase from 122.6 million in 1990 to 147.2 million in 2005, an increase of 25 million from 1990 to 2005. (See Figures 11 and 12.) Information on the changing demographics of the labor force will be given in the section that follows.

LABOR FORCE PROFILE

Demographic data reflect a changing profile for the U.S. population. By the year 2000, immigrants and minorities will

Figure 11

EMPLOYMENT CHANGES IN MAJOR SERVICE-PRODUCING AREAS

(numbers in millions)

Industry	1975	1990	2005	1975–2005
Transportation/ Communications/Utilities	4.5	5.8	6.7	0.9
Wholesale	4.4	6.2	7.2	1.0
Retail	12.6	19.7	24.8	5.1
Finance/Insurance/ Real Estate	4.2	6.7	8.1	1.4
Services	13.6	27.6	39.1	11.5
Government	14.7	18.3	21.5	3.2

account for a larger share of the U.S. population than they do today, according to the Bureau of Labor Statistics. The U.S. is becoming more and more multicultural, which has a significant impact on the labor force. Immigrants, generally, are of working age and differ from the U.S. population in educational and occupational backgrounds. This means an increase in the working age population and a decrease in the older group. Immigrants, minority groups, and women account for 85 percent of all new entrants into the work force.

Many new challenges have arisen that employers must face. First, there is a gap between employees' skills and company's skill requirements. To overcome this, some companies are developing remedial programs that include language and writing skills. How are these concerns being addressed? In a study called *Workforce 2000: Work and Workers for the 21st Century* by the Hudson Institute and the U.S. Department of Labor, the findings revealed that 42 percent of the respondents were engaged in

Figure 12

EMPLOYMENT BY MAJOR OCCUPATIONAL GROUP

1990-2005

(numbers in millions)

Occupation	1990		2005		% Change
	No.	%	No.	%	1990–2005
Administrative support	22.0	17.9	24.8	16.9	13.1
Professional specialty	15.8	12.9	20.9	14.2	32.3
Marketing and sales	14.1	11.5	17.5	11.9	24.1
Service occupations	19.2	15.7	24.8	16.9	29.2

"explicit minority recruitment." Some of these firms are providing programs in which managers are trained to value diversity (29 percent) or in which minorities are trained for supervisory positions (12 percent). (See Figure 13.)

Second, organizations need to understand and learn about the diversified backgrounds of this potential market for employees, as well as appreciate the differences in language, gender, skills, and cultural values and customs. Executives and employees need to learn new ways of interacting with and embracing different behaviors of people in a diverse work force. Acting on the issues mentioned above and developing strategies and programs to learn how to deal with these issues are the keys to an organization's effectiveness and success.

Third, advanced technology increasingly leads to the need for a skilled work force that is becoming more specialized. Predictions indicate that by the year 2000, three out of four jobs will be ones that do not even exist today.

Figure 13

PROGRAMS FOR MANAGING CULTURAL DIVERSITY

Program	% of Respondents
Training Managers to Value Diversity	29%
Training Minorities for Supervisory Positions	12%
Sponsoring Minority Support Groups	11%
Sponsoring Mentoring Programs	10%
Courses on English as a Second Language	9%

MODIFICATIONS IN COMPANY PRACTICES

Company policies and practices are also changing in an effort to cope with the labor shortages and accompanying skills gap. The *Workforce 2000* report indicates some of these changes. For example, 50 percent of the respondents now offer flextime, and 48 percent of the companies are using employee attitude surveys. Other areas now being developed include supervisory training in worker autonomy, job sharing, self-managed work teams, productivity incentives, compressed workweek, and gain sharing. The percentages run higher for companies with quality improvement programs. (See Figure 14.)

TELECOMMUTING

Computer terminals, modems, and advanced telephone technology have made telecommuting possible. In essence, this is a home/office computing connection and is a new approach to managing workers and the workflow. The different designations

Figure 14

WORKPLACE PRACTICES AND POLICIES

Practice	*% of Respondents*
Flextime	50%
Employee attitude surveys	48%
Part-time work force	48%
Employee involvement teams	33%
Supervisory training in worker autonomy	28%
Productivity incentives for middle management	28%
Job sharing	21%
Self-managed work teams	12%

by which this concept is known are cottage industry, electronic cottage, teleworking by electronic service, the flexiplace, and worksteading. Employees, instead of working at home, may also work in small satellite offices or in an executive business center where clients have an office and conference room as well as some service. This basic method for working outside of the office is not new to those individuals who are "out in the field" selling, consulting, or rendering customer service. What has happened is that many more employees in different job classifications can now function productively on the outside, a fact made possible by advanced technology and communications. Jonathan Goodrich in "Telecommuting in America" states that approximately 350 firms in the U.S. have a telecommuting program that involves from a few to more than 100 employees. Approximately 3.4 million employees work at home for a company while some 16 million, or 14 percent, of the U.S. civilian labor force, work at home either after hours or as a second source of income. One such job would be to handle catalog sales and take orders right in your own home. Other related major telecommuting occupations are travel agents, insurance agents, purchasing agents, applications processors, and marketing managers. The advantages of working at home, according to a survey of more than 2,000 adults are shown in Figure 15.

The drawbacks, mostly with supplies and equipment (51 percent), family interruptions (38 percent), and mixing work and family life (37 percent) are reflected in Figure 16.

If you are interested in the sales aspect of customer service, then telecommuting might interest you. According to Goodrich, DuPont has over a thousand sales managers and representatives teleworking; Pacific Bell has more than 200 teleworkers, basically sales and service personnel; and Beneficial Finance uses telecommuting to improve customer service, among other services. Companies telework as a means of providing quality service to customers within a faster period of time. For example, via the computer terminal, orders can be transmitted instantaneously to a central location so that delivery to customers can be expedited.

Telecommuting is not for everyone. As you read the statistics, you should realize that there are advantages and disadvantages to telecommuting. Individuals have to determine their preferences as to whether they prefer to work at home or in a structured environment. So, consider your options wisely.

TEMPORARY EMPLOYEES

Modern businesses and industries now see using temps as a management tool, whereas in previous decades temporary personnel were used as fill-ins when regular employees were out ill

Figure 15

ADVANTAGES OF TELECOMMUTING

Item	*% of Respondents*
More control of one's work schedule	53%
Wear more confortable clothes	36%
Avoid commuting	35%
Not have a boss close by	28%
Able to care for children	20%
No interruptions from coworkers	20%
Job seems more like work	20%
Not minding overtime as much	15%

Figure 16

DISADVANTAGES OF TELECOMMUTING

Item	*% of Respondents*
Not having necessary supplies or equipment	51%
Too many family interruptions	38%
Over mixing work and family life	37%
Distractions by household chores	32%
Lack of interaction with colleagues	27%
Lack of regular routine	23%
Difficult to quit after a full day	16%
Work done at home is less important	14%

or on vacation, when a special project had a deadline, or during peak periods. The recessionary economy and mushrooming labor costs have expanded the concept of temporary help to include long- as well as short-term employment. The recession has also affected the supply and demand of temp workers. There are more temps than jobs to fill.

Temporary jobs do exist in customer service. This type of employment is attractive to individuals who are returning to school to gain knowledge and skills, who are enrolled in degree programs, and who have lost their jobs and want to earn money until they find employment in their chosen field of work.

Temporary employment provides an opportunity to work in different environments with diverse responsibilities. In addition to salary, temporary employees may now receive health benefits, insurance, child care, and even retirement plan choices. Olsten temporary agency is an example of a company that has a tax withholding and reimbursement child care plan for its employees. Presently, employment agencies are giving personality, general aptitude, and skills tests in math, English, and the computer.

During periods of economic recession, the trend in the firm is to understaff full-time employees and hire temporary workers when needed. The company reduces its weekly payroll by not having to pay a guaranteed wage during slack periods, nor does it pay for employee benefits. In customer service positions, this is not always most desirable to the customer, because a customer-employee relationship that had been developed is suddenly dissolved. Nevertheless, this is an alternative work pattern that might serve your needs.

CHAPTER 5

INDUSTRY PROFILES

Quality and service are becoming passwords for survival in our competitive society. How are some of the companies responding to this? What are some of their practices? How does one company differ from another? How are they meeting the challenge of providing superior customer service? This chapter will profile several industries to give you some insight into structure and practices. Information was gathered from various sources; interviews, meetings at company sites, annual reports, company printed materials, and professional literature. Wherever possible, a brief profile was given of a specific company.

MANUFACTURING

POLAROID CORPORATION

Located in Cambridge, Massachusetts, Polaroid is an international firm that designs, manufactures, and markets worldwide a variety of products in instant image recording fields, such as photographic cameras and films, magnetic media, filters, and lenses. Their products are used in personal photography, industry, science, medicine, and education.

Edwin H. Land, founder of the company, in a 1980 letter to shareholders wrote that a program should not be undertaken "unless the goal is manifestly important and its achievement nearly impossible. Do not do anything that anyone else can do readily." He believed that by working together, individuals could perform the impossible. The *1990 Annual Report* indicates that Polaroid had a profitable year and showed growth.

However, this year of success was not translated by the Chairman and Vice Chairman of the Board, nor by the President and Chief Executive Officer, as a reason for being content and merely continuing to conduct business as usual. Their goals for the future require change in the corporate and organizational structures, particularly with its renewed focus on the customer and quality. Their products, as developed, will be sensitive to customers' needs and will exceed their expectations. A better understanding of the market and trends and the ability to respond more quickly to market changes is a major goal of the organization.

In past decades, a firm that had a good product was usually successful. Currently, with global competition and a more sophisticated consumer, the above statement is no longer true. Polaroid believes that technology combined with customer needs and expectations is the key. Therefore, they are incorporating customer feedback at every step of product development and the manufacturing process.

To achieve a "maximum level of product and service quality for our customers," in 1990 Polaroid initiated a Total Quality Ownership program that involves every member of the company and as a reward includes financial incentives. The philosophy of the company is to encourage and enable all members of the firm to do their very best work so that the expectations of every customer, every time, can be met. Their plan of action seeks to "improve communication and collaboration, share decision-making, and establish clear, objective measures for tracking customer satisfaction." Employees are rewarded for additional knowledge gained and applied, and for participation in work redesign by assuming multiskilled and cross-functional work assignments that often result in savings, revenue gains, and quality improvements. Motivational programs include boat cruises, divisional softball games, summer cookouts, and attendance at national meetings.

To qualify for a job at Polaroid as a customer service representative, an entry-level position, a high school education is the minimum requirement. Candidates need to demonstrate strong interpersonal skills, good communication skills that include listening and effective use of English, and the ability to learn and understand basic technical concepts. An employee can advance to the position of customer service associate or customer service specialist. These positions would include more staff responsibilities, handling specific projects and service programs, and leading/supervising customer service representatives.

Training is given to all new employees with extensive follow-up, and on-going internal and external programs are available. Testing to determine qualifications of a candidate is administered through writing exercises, interviews, telephone contact, and role playing.

The Polaroid Service Mission reads: "To promote the greater use of and satisfaction with Polaroid products; and to be a resource for the corporation on product performance and consumer attitudes."

IBM

Always known to be a giant in the field of computers and office equipment, IBM was founded in 1914 by Thomas J. Watson. His business philosophy was based on three principles: respect for individuals, the best possible customer service, and the pursuit of superior performance—zero defects in products and services. Included in these principles were rewards for superior performance, promotions from within, and a democratic environment—no titles on doors or executive washrooms. According to John Akers in the May 1991 issue of *Quality Progress,* these principles provided the platform upon which IBM developed a very successful business.

IBM's strategy for growth, as stated in the *1990 Annual Report,* is "to provide customers with the best solutions; to strengthen the competitiveness of our products and services; and to improve our efficiency." In essence, IBM was responsible to its employees and committed to its customers and society. However, evaluations of how well IBM was fulfilling this obligation reflected that they were losing ground with other service providers, as indicated in *IBM Update,* June/July 1990. More on this will be discussed in the section under "The New IBM."

In 1990, IBM intensified its focus on customers and initiated Market-Driven Quality so that it is more customer-responsive and more productive. This has become a #1 priority to the company in order to enable it to compete in the information processing industry. Some ways in which IBM expects to achieve this are through more visitations to customers' offices, more marketing, and more service people. Also, international marketing executives were appointed in each geographic region to coordinate marketing, service, and support activities for international customers. The three basic components of this market-driven quality effort, as reported in the 1990 issue of *Electronic*

Business, are the following: (1) defining market needs, eliminating defects, achieving quicker response time, empowering employees, and measuring progress; (2) analyzing business processes; and (3) measuring quality.

Another challenge occurred when IBM Rochester did not win the first Malcolm Baldrige National Quality Award. Determined to achieve it, they took stock of their weak area, which was mainly the need to "facilitate communication between the site and the customer"; they developed a new strategy to correct the problem, thus closing the loop between the laboratory, manufacturing, and the customer. In 1990, they won the Malcolm Baldrige Award.

Heavy investments in education and training have always been a part of IBM's strategy. Employees receive training and education from the very first day they join the company. It is given both formally in the classroom and informally on the job through their entire career. More than $1 billion a year are invested in education; and on any particular day, in excess of 20,000 people are taking classes. This is considered necessary because of the changing pace of technology and the changing nature of customers' needs. By educating people, you also empower them. They learn to use their creativity in satisfying customers.

The New IBM. In the December 16, 1991, issue of *Business Week,* Chairman John Akers unfolded a bold plan for redefining the business in an effort to restore the illustrious position IBM once held. Dozens of semi-independent operations would be created; each division would have more autonomy; heads of the new units would act as CEOs; employees at all levels would have to produce; decision-making, including pricing, would occur within each unit; managers would be measured against profit goals; and each division would seek new markets.

Undoubtedly, IBM will continue to sponsor its many community programs in the U.S. for women, minorities, and handicapped persons. In Canada, as well as in the U.S., IBM has invested heavily in education, primarily for kindergarten through grade 12.

The service, PC, workstation, and software markets have a long-term growth potential. Will IBM regain the position it once held at the forefront of one of the world's most dynamic industries? In terms of employment, there will still be a broad range of opportunities at IBM. Jobs in marketing, a major area of opportunity, are available in over 200 cities. Marketing employees are the first line of contact between IBM and the customer. The position of *marketing representative* is basically a face-to-face customer assignment in the branch office environment. Marketing representatives have primary responsibility for an account (or accounts) and for high-level customer contact. They develop solutions to customer problems, establish short- and long-range plans, initiate and develop account strategies, and participate in installation planning.

Education at the company is continuous in intensive on-the-job or formal training. There is even a marketing education center in Atlanta. At the end of a training period, personnel are assigned to a position as a junior member of an account team or to a number of small-to-medium customers in a specified territory. There is flexibility in deciding on a career path. Initially someone may follow a route as a marketing representative and then decide to take the management route. In a marketing environment, team selling is strongly emphasized. External programs are encouraged, which should contribute to an employee's effectiveness and promotability. Employees may take courses or pursue degree programs through IBM's Tuition Refund Plan.

MAIL-ORDER FIRMS

LILLIAN VERNON CORPORATION

With corporate headquarters in Mt. Vernon, New York, Lillian Vernon Corporation is a 40-year-old specialty catalog company that markets gift, household, gardening, decorative, and children's products. They are committed to quality and customer satisfaction. During fiscal 1991, they mailed over 120 million core catalogs, 8 million home catalogs, 16 million sale catalogs, and during the fall of 1990 added the "Lilly's Kids" catalog. During fiscal 1992, eighteen editions of their catalogs will be distributed, with a circulation of over 136 million. To give you an idea of the volume of business, in fiscal 1991 4.3 million orders were shipped. The products are primarily sold through direct marketing, and catalogs are targeted to meet the needs of their customers.

How is Lillian Vernon meeting the needs of their customers? Offerings in the sale catalogs will be expanded in response to demand for practical products and good values; items are personalized at no extra charge to customer; traditional product lines are sold at substantial savings; fast response time is met in reaction to changes in trends, tastes, and interests; and products exclusive to Lillian Vernon are offered. To determine customers' changing needs, the company has focus groups, conducts customer surveys, and performs a careful analysis of their data base, which has over 12 million names. Over 90 percent of their customers are working women with children and an average income of over $48,000.

The catalog industry will continue to grow. Increasing numbers of women are entering the labor force and have greater disposal income with less time to shop.

MACBEAT

A relatively new mail-order company, MacBeat, came into existence during 1989 in Santa Fe, New Mexico. They sell fully supported products (hardware and software) and services for musicians who use the MacIntosh line of computers; they also serve as an information source for the latest developments in the area of music on the Mac. The products they sell are used and completely understood by MacBeat owners and staff.

The customer is the most important cog in the firm, and the customer must be foremost in mind when conducting business. The firm serves their customers in a variety of ways. First, for a visual impression, their catalogs are designed and produced on the software programs they market. Each item is thoroughly defined, particularly valuable for the beginner. These explanations are given with appropriate analogies. Second, to break the monotony, humorous asides are included in the text occasionally. Third, Music Accelerators, which are basically comprehensive tutorials to help the learner, keep the software user-friendly and make the material easier to understand. For example, there are learning guides which include charts, a glossary of terms written in plain English and with helpful diagrams, and Composer's Tips with accompanying diskette. A software program, "Compose Yourself," is a thorough guide on how to compose. Fourth, the firm does troubleshooting and has a toll-free number. Fifth, suggestions from readers are solicited; and sixth, the firm custom configures items like racks, tables, and stands on which to support the equipment and programs.

A person who wants to work in customer service and who enjoys music and computers might be interested in employment opportunities in this type of field. The owner of this business does have musical abilities, but no formal business background.

To be successful on the job, he indicated that you do need the following skills:

- Oral communication skills—the ability to handle the telephone, answer ads, and ask for information;
- Marketing/sales skills;
- Personal skills—establishing rapport on the telephone, developing a connection on the telephone;
- Attitudes—is sincere, is honest, and has integrity;
- Organizational skills;
- Attention to detail.

The benefits of working for a small firm differ from that of a large firm. See Chapter 8 for a full discussion.

RETAILING

LEVITZ FURNITURE CORPORATION

Levitz operates a chain of over 120 furniture showrooms in 25 states throughout the nation, with its corporate headquarters in Boca Raton, Florida. The company is dedicated to providing excellent service to its customers and to replacing defective merchandise. Levitz communicates this philosophy in a 4 1/2″ x 9″ customer folder in which it outlines its "10–Point Customer Bill of Rights" statement. Included within this folder are booklets that are helpful to the consumer when making purchases, such as a glossary of furniture terms, how to select fabric, how to assist a furniture salesperson in helping the customer, and a feedback questionnaire card. As stated in Levitz's "10 Point Customer Bill of Rights," the customer has the right to:

1. Expect Courteous, Responsive Treatment. Customer service receives top priority at Levitz.
2. Expect Furniture Shopping to be Pleasant.
3. Utmost Selection and Instant Availability.
4. A Choice of the Way You Buy Furniture. You may take it with you and avoid delivery charges or pay for delivery.
5. Purchase Items at the Advertised Price.
6. Expect Quality Merchandise at Low Prices. To accomplish this, the warehouse/showroom is housed under one roof.
7. Be Satisfied with Your Purchase. A "Service Pledge" is printed on all sales transactions, which is given to the consumer when the purchase is made.
8. Quality Performance from Your Purchase.
9. Credit Consideration on Your Purchase. A payment plan for purchases may be arranged, and the customer may ask for a pre-approved line of credit for future purchases.
10. Be Heard. A consumer toll-free line is available when a problem cannot be resolved at the local level. A local manager then gets the report, and a return call to the customer can be expected within one to three days.

UTILITIES

CONSOLIDATED EDISON COMPANY OF NEW YORK, INC.

Con Ed supplies electric service in New York City (except part of Queens) and most of Westchester County. It also supplies gas in Manhattan, the Bronx, and parts of Queens and Westchester, and steam in part of Manhattan. Con Ed's corporate headquarters in Manhattan had 19,483 employees as of December 31, 1990.

As reported in the *1990 Annual Report,* the Branch staff maintains approximately 143,313 accounts, or 222,498 electric and gas meters. Responsibilities include monthly meter readings; turn-on and turn-off service upon customer request; maintenance of account records; handling customer telephone, mail, and in-person inquiries; collection of bills; and routine payment processing. Staff members identify procedures that no longer respond to current customer needs and are involved in interdepartmental work committees to ensure effective action.

The three departments at this branch are the following:

1. Meter Operations—concerned with field-directed activities affecting meters as well as credit and collection activities;
2. Account Responsibility—maintenance and response to customer telephone and mail inquiries; and
3. Business Office—handles customer inquiries and processes delivered payments.

Con Ed sponsors many free consumer education programs, some of which are enumerated as follows:

- Energy Services is a new department that was recently created to get new customers on-line quickly, to resolve service problems, and to promote and implement the company's energy-efficiency and economic incentive programs.
- CONCERN is a program designed for seniors, handicapped people, and special needs customers.
- Bills are printed in larger type and in Braille for the visually impaired.
- On-the-spot translation of telephone conversations into other languages is now in progress. This program will be helpful to those individuals who are not well versed in English.

- An Energy Conservation Program was developed by Con Ed in 1991. It offered compact fluorescent bulbs to all residential customers at a steep discount.
- A host of videotapes on healthy living, the environment, safety, career development, and conservation are available to schools and adult groups.
- Consumer education representatives are available for presentations.

For the personal and professional development of its employees, many training programs have been created. They are designed for the many levels of employees who work for Con Ed. Some courses appropriate for customer service employees are: Business Writing Fundamentals, Listening Skills, Reading Dynamics, Team Building, Self-Management, Communication Workshop, Managing Your Time, and Presentation Skills.

If you are interested in working for a utility, the customer service positions that are available are enumerated below:

Customer Service Managers answer telephone calls and letters, handle customer accounts, check and retrieve records from databases.

Clerks file, record, and log in work; send information to terminals; scan customer letters and send them to computer.

Customer Field Representatives read the meters.

Customer Service Representatives set up routes, track work, develop forms. The distinction between customer service representative and senior customer service representative is narrowing because of the automated functions now performed.

Account Analysts maintain account records and check their accuracy.

Credit Analysts collect delinquent bills.

Telephone Account Representatives handle accounts over the phone.

District Office Account Representatives handle customer accounts at walk-in branch locations.

Project Managers now total twenty-six employees at Con Ed who deal in customer service. They respond to telephone calls, communicate in writing, handle the customer accounts and database.

Con Ed is trying to leap into the next century through the use of technology. They now have an automatic mapping system of each area. It is relatively simple to look at a picture of a particular branch, designate routes, and indicate priority orders. The customer field representatives use hand-held computers, which upon input immediately updates system. Interestingly, a prompting system is a component, and relevant questions about the customer's account are asked. A message might also flash which asks for a verification.

CREDIT CARD SERVICES

The competition in the credit card business is growing keener. No longer can a company sell just a card. The delivery of customer service is a major factor in the recruitment and retention of members. They must also design innovative service programs as an edge against the fluctuations of the economy.

AMERICAN EXPRESS

As one of the major companies known for its excellent and innovative service, the greatest strength of American Express is its commitment to serving the customer. The Chairman of the Board and Chief Quality Officer is known for stating that the three most important factors in the success of the company are quality, quality, and quality. The first two guiding principles of the organization, which are clearly set forth on a pocket-size card, support this statement. They read, "The marketplace is the driving force behind all we do," and "Outstanding customer service is both our greatest competitive strength and our overriding commitment."

One of the ways in which American Express provides superior service is through a national toll-free number for credit card holders, as well as a local number in some areas, such as New York City. The company also takes the role of intermediary between cardholder and vendor when charges on the monthly statement show inaccuracies or are questioned. Payment of such a charge is held in abeyance until a satisfactory response is submitted by the vendor to both American Express and the cardholder. Service is also rendered through timeliness of action; quick authorizations of charges; no established limit of credit for members who pay their bills; expeditious replacement of lost or stolen cards; and access to the company twenty-four hours a day, year round, worldwide.

The company conducts considerable market research to determine what their customers value. Based on the findings, they design the service. They also develop a pattern of each consumer's spending so that if excesses are shown on a particular account, the company places a call to verify the bill and/or to determine if the card was lost.

What are the customer service positions at American Express? The two main branches in customer service are the telephone service representatives and the correspondence representatives. Cross-training enables these employees to move back and forth between the two areas of responsibility, depending on need. Grades have been established for different levels of employment. The logical career path would be to advance from a senior telephone service representative, then to supervisor, and ultimately to manager. Since the ratio of managers to staff is approximately one to eighty or a hundred, this level would be more difficult to achieve than the supervisory level, whose ratio is approximately one to twenty.

On the correspondence side, analysts and bill adjusters are entry-level positions at three grade levels. The difference between these two positions is that the analyst needs to work with in-house data that are available, while the adjuster needs to contact card members or service establishments to research information to help resolve a problem. Senior positions also exist in this section, and advancement would be to a supervisory or managerial position. Employees can also move laterally into credit and collection services.

What are some of the qualifications that the company looks for in a candidate for employment? Most important is that the individual has to be service oriented. Applicants need to speak well, have a good telephone voice, be motivated, able to handle themselves well, and able to think on their feet. On the correspondence side, writing skills are necessary. In terms of educational background, a college education is generally preferred.

For advancement, a demonstrated competency in performance of job is measured by productivity and quality. For example, a correspondence representative would be measured by the number of letters answered per hour, and the evaluation of quality would be based on accuracy. American Express has very stringent standards on quality: Only 98 percent and above is acceptable. The performance of a telephone service representative would be measured by accuracy and the number of calls handled per hour. Generally, an employee is expected to handle twenty calls an hour and should be ready to do so 97 percent of their time. An automatic call distributor records time spent on each call, when the employee left the work station, and so on.

Senior employees perform evaluations which are used in reports for internal checks and for performance reviews. A member of the Quality Assurance Department also conducts evaluations that are incorporated in official reports to be sent to senior management.

The company makes a considerable investment in each employee's training. Telephone service individuals might receive from six to eight weeks of daily formal classroom training and correspondence employees, twelve to fourteen weeks. This is followed up with an equal amount of time on the job under very close supervision and "hand-holding." It generally takes nine months for employees to reach the top of the curve. Retraining also occurs annually to instruct personnel on changes in policies and procedures, new program installations, and changing technology.

Training in the past usually signalled learning new equipment or how to navigate a system. However, American Express periodically reviews their course offerings to determine if employees are taught to be service-oriented people rather than solely transaction oriented. Their ultimate goal is to make their customers friends for life. Learning how to say things and to use the right words is very important, especially in areas such as credit and collections.

How can employees change their behaviors? American Express has a variety of motivational and recognition programs to inspire their workers. Probably the most prestigious program is called Great Performers. Periodically, employees are recommended who have rendered exceptional customer service, far beyond what is expected. The facts are verified, and the winners are selected. The victors are flown in from around the world, and some of the awards might be a week's vacation, a Great Performers certificate and pin, an awards banquet, and perhaps even a sum of money in traveler's checks.

At the corporate level, another program is the Chairman's Award for Quality. Teams of people from different disciplines work together on a project to find a creative solution to a business issue that affects quality. If the outcome shows great success, the team is recognized by the Chairman of the Board and significant amounts of money are awarded.

Within the Operating Center, points are given each month for attendance, productivity, and quality. A prize for the maximum number of points might be a trip to Bermuda or some other exciting vacation spot. Each department within the operating Center has a program called Rock Stars, in which an employee might be recognized for excellent work, such as handling telephone calls exceptionally well. The importance of this is apparent when you realize that customer service personnel spend approximately ninety percent of their time on the telephone and ten percent on correspondence.

American Express is an aggressive company that encourages the entrepreneurial spirit among its employees. Staff is encouraged to be innovative, to take risks, and to constantly seek ways of improving the job being done. For individuals looking for employment in customer service, the following statement from one of the employees at the managerial level at American Express is sound advice for a beginner: "Find something that you think will grow and is not fully mature yet. Add value to it and grow with it."

BANKING

The world of banking is an exciting field. Banking operations have expanded tremendously in recent years and now cover—in addition to savings deposits and loans—financial planning, brokerage services, money market investments, and ancillary services such as Keogh plans and IRAs. Unlike the services banks gave years ago, today everything has a price, for this generates income.

Banking is a field where opportunities exist for individuals from different educational backgrounds. In banking, customer service employees have many and varied responsibilities, depending on the institution where the individual is employed and the type of banking services rendered. The information that follows reflects realistic experiences of an individual who worked at both a commercial bank and a savings bank and whose experience ranged from teller, to customer service representative, to manager, and ultimately to vice president.

An entry-level position is usually that of a teller. A customer service representative performs every task a teller does except handle the cash. In this position at a savings and loan institution, you would be servicing individual customers, opening accounts, doing proof sheets at the end of the day for checks and transfers, explaining bank services and procedures, rolling over CDs, and selling bonds and traveler's checks. In a commercial bank, you would set up wire transfers, stop payments, certify checks, process pension accounts, handle passbook loans, and investigate customer complaints. Selling has become an important part of the responsibilities of the job, too. For example, if a customer has a savings account, the customer service representative might suggest opening up a checking account, becoming a credit card carrier, or buying a CD. Along with a complete bank package might come some complimentary services, such as reduced auto loan rates or a credit card without an annual charge.

Banks are paternalistic to their employees, and they are interested in career paths. An entry-level position can be obtained with a college degree; however, in order to move up the ladder, you must continue your education. One career move that you can easily make after working as a customer service representative is to move up to a local branch manager.

The American Institute of Banking is a facility for further study in the area. The banks themselves have training programs for the various levels of personnel, and it is not uncommon for a branch operations supervisor to be admitted to a management training program.

If you wish to find employment in customer service in the banking industry, be prepared to take integrity, math, and general knowledge tests. If you score well and your interview is good, then you will probably be recommended for a position. The customer service representative in a banking environment is highly visible, and it is a career track. You usually have your own telephone extension as well as inscribed business cards and memo pads. Part-time employment is also available in banking institutions. Thus, there is a great deal of flexibility in the field of banking.

W. Anthony Turner, in "Many Banks Arc Seeking Help in Sales," states that with the increase in brokerage operations at many banks, new opportunities are available for people with sales or financial backgrounds. "Banks were working to create their own types of sales cultures, now geared more toward building relationships than simply promoting products.'' He further states that banks are attempting to ''draw their customers away from doing business with brokerage firms.'' Lincoln Savings Bank in New York established a private banking unit a year ago staffed by several registered representatives who make customer contacts and then transfer them to the bank's brokerage unit. Many banks use outside training specialists to conduct workshops for these employees.

POTPOURRI OF OTHER
CUSTOMER SERVICE IDEAS

One hotel chain is giving ''empowerment training'' to approximately 70,000 employees along with which goes the right to make decisions when guest problems arise. Since hiring an employee with a customer-service orientation is so important, at an entertainment facility, candidates for jobs are interviewed in groups of three so that their interaction with one another is clearly visible. A high-tech firm uses a procedure in which a customer service rep who is unable to respond to a customer's question routes the call to an expert who can. This same expert must then report back to the rep within two hours to confirm that the customer has been satisfied. This same rep is also required to make three outgoing calls per day to customers with whom he had contact within the past day or two. The rep normally asks if the customer got what was called for and if there was anything else the company could do.

SURVEY OF CUSTOMER
SERVICE EMPLOYEES

The companies in the industry profiles given above were not included in the findings of the 1991 survey that was conducted by the author. Respondents were customer service personnel employed in manufacturing, commercial, retailing, and financial organizations. The commonly used title is customer service representative. Another title indicated is the claims and returns assistant who is an employee who processes claims, issues credit or writes a denial letter, and handles authorization reports and logs. Some of the positions to which an employee could advance are customer service associate, customer service specialist, international customer service representative, customer service area manager, and senior customer service representative.

Other findings of the study are indicated below:

- Generally, a high school education is the minimum educational level for an applicant, but a degree is preferred or the equivalency in experience.
- Courses of study that are desirable are business, communications, and psychology. This is understandable because of the interrelationships between customer and employee.
- Candidates should possess strong interpersonal skills, listening ability, and good communication skills; they should be articulate, energetic, hard working, and innovative. Skills and knowledge required by the employing firm are organization, prioritization, strong and effective use of English, the ability to learn and understand basic technical concepts, problem-solving skills, telephone skills, written communication skills, and computer literacy.

- The basic criteria for promotional opportunities include skill development and application, a good attitude, being a team player, and good work habits.
- Testing procedures vary from role-playing situations to written exercises, to panel interviews.
- Practically all of the firms have designed motivational and/or employee recognition programs such as boat cruises, summer cookouts, divisional softball games, bonuses, incentives, employee recognition month, team recognition, and attendance at national meetings.
- Formal and informal training programs, both internally and externally, are given. New employees receive in-depth training on systems, operations, and product line; staff receive regular updates.
- Most of the service rendered is face-to-face and over the telephone.

The following excerpt on company philosophy, as stated by one respondent, indicates the service-oriented direction many firms are now taking.

". . . to add value to our products through quality service that meets or exceeds customer expectations while supporting and enhancing sales and marketing strategies."

CHAPTER 6

EDUCATIONAL PREPARATION FOR CUSTOMER SERVICE POSITIONS

The workplace of the 1990s is different from that of previous decades. Within the diversity of industries and professions, many uncertainties exist. However, there is one absolute direction: "The customer is always right!" The common thread in every position, no matter how varied the responsibilities are from firm to firm, is that the customer comes first and must be served. Therefore, educational and employee development programs need to focus on the skills, knowledge, and personal qualities that are required for customer service personnel. According to Rebecca Gatlin and Kerry Gatlin in "Emphasizing Customer Service," employees must learn to "appreciate the importance of customer service as a competitive strategy." By providing outstanding service, speed, reliability, and friendliness, the likelihood is that your firm will receive a top rating in the minds of the customers.

PROGRAMS OF STUDY

Education for customer service is available at many levels, ranging from vocational training programs to universities. The International Customer Service Association undertook a study to investigate formal education requirements for customer service in colleges and universities. Twenty-five courses generally found in university business curriculums were surveyed for both customer service non-management and management employees.

The findings revealed that courses dealing with human behavior and interpersonal communication generally were rated higher than quantitative subjects, such as accounting and economics. Decision-making concepts and business writing were ranked very high for both groups. As expected, courses in management and supervision for customer service management employees were deemed more important for management employees than non-management employees, while courses in sales and marketing were rated high for both groups. The asterisks next to courses shown in Figures 17 and 18 indicate that these courses were ranked within the top ten most important course requirements for both managerial and non-managerial positions in customer service. The investigation conducted to compare differences in course requirements between manufacturing firms and service providers showed that the same college background would prepare a student for either type of firm.

In a two-year course of study, students can earn an Associate in Applied Science (A.A.S.) degree in a marketing curriculum. A typical program is shown below, which appears in a recent catalog of the State University of New York College of Technology at Alfred.

Marketing

A.A.S. Degree

First Year

		First				Second	
BUS	1023	Bus Orgn & Mgt	3	ACCT	2223	Managerial Acctg	3
ACCT	1123	Financial Acctg	3	BUS	2033	Bus Commun	3
DATA	1003	Intro Bus Sys Micr	3	LIT	2603	Intro to Lit	3
COMP	1503	Fr . Compo-sition II	3	SPEECH	2083	Effective Speaking	3
*MATH			3	MKT	2073	Prin Market	3
HPE		Physical Ed		MATH*		or	
						Science	3
		Hrs.	15			Hrs.	18

Second Year

		Third				Fourth	
BUS	3043	Business Law I	3	BUS	4053	Business Law II	3
MKT	1063	Salesmanship	3	MKT	3113	Consumer Behavior	3
MKT	1033	Advertising Prin	3	MKT	4123	Mrktg Research OR	
ECON	1013	Prin Econ I	3	MKT	4143	Indus Marketing	3
		*Free Elective	3	ECON	2023	Prin Econ II	3
		Hrs.	15			Bus or Tech Elective	3
						Hrs.	15

Figure 17

RATING OF COLLEGE COURSES FOR
CUSTOMER SERVICE NON-MANAGEMENT EMPLOYEES

Course	Percentage Important/Very Important
Persuasion*	77%
Decision-Making Concepts*	72%
Business Writing*	71%
Negotiation Concepts*	66%
Salesmanship*	65%
Marketing Concepts*	50%
Management Information Systems*	48%
Organizational Behavior*	47%
Consumerism	39%
Inventory	38%
Business Psychology	35%
Transportation	34%
Business Management Concepts	29%
Accounting	24%
Supervision Concepts	22%
Manufacturing	22%
Financial Concepts	17%
Economics	16%
Business Law	16%
Market Research	16%
International Business	16%
Forecasting	15%
Advertising	14%
Business Statistics	13%
Retail Management	11%

Figure 18

RATING OF COLLEGE COURSES FOR
MANAGEMENT EMPLOYEES

Course	Percentage Important/Very Important
Business Management Concepts	96%
Supervision Concepts	95%
Decision-Making Concepts*	95%
Business Writing*	91%
Organizational Behavior*	91%
Persuasion*	87%
Management Information Systems*	87%
Marketing Concepts*	87%
Negotiation Concepts*	86%
Salesmanship*	77%
Business Psychology	73%
Forecasting	67%
Consumerism	67%
Financial Concepts	67%
Business Statistics	60%
Accounting	57%
Economics	57%
Inventory	54%
Market Research	50%
Transportation	50%
Business Law	47%
Manufacturing	44%
International Business	39%
Advertising	38%
Retail Management	33%

Below are excerpts from several course descriptions in the State University at Alfred catalog which directly relate to customer service.

Principles of Marketing. An introductory course in the field of marketing with particular attention given to the marketing functions and institutions as they pertain to the product, price, place and promotion aspects of bringing goods and services to the consumer.

Consumer Behavior. Attention is given to the basic determinants of consumer behavior, consumer purchasing strategy, interpersonal environmental influences, and the influence of the business environment upon consumer purchasing decisions.

Retail Management. An examination of the current problems in retail management. Designed to familiarize the student with techniques used to identify and understand the existence of needs of the consumer market.

Industrial Marketing. An overall view of the marketing of industrial goods and services at the manufacturing and middleman level is presented. Subject areas include: product planning and development; marketing intelligence; management of the sales force; industrial advertising and sales promotion; customer service and the industrial buying process.

At a lower level, among the many skills training programs that exist, there are courses of study that lead to becoming a customer service representative. Some programs require a high school diploma or GED certificate; others don't insist on a high school diploma but have a GED component built into the education and training. Eligibility varies, since some of the vocational resources are funded under the Job Training Partnership Act.

The New York City Department of Employment, under the Economic Dislocation and Worker's Adjustment Assistance Act (EDWAAA) is funding many retraining programs for dislocated workers so that they can reenter the labor force. In order to qualify, an individual must have become unemployed as a result of a layoff or closing of a firm, have been unemployed for more than 15 weeks, or have limited employment opportunities in a similar occupation, or be a displaced homemaker because of the loss of a primary source of income. Individuals accepted into these programs receive stipends for transportation and lunch. Supportive services are provided. The education is job-related and includes techniques for finding a job.

One such program site is the Skills Enhancement Center at Bronx Community College, under the directorship of William Ross. Students go through a rigorous classroom training program for twenty weeks, from 8:30 A.M. to 3:30 P.M., after which graduates are assisted in job placement. In addition to meeting the JTPA/EDWAAA eligibility standards and being between the ages of 22 and 59, the entry requirements for the ''Customer Service/Health Services Representative'' include an eighth- to twelfth-grade reading and math level, finger and manual dexterity, good oral communication skills, motivation, and demonstrated initiative during a panel interview. Upon completion of the program, students are expected to achieve the following objectives:

- To communicate orally by phone and in person;
- To handle inquiries and complaints; to exchange and convey information; and to provide direction and offer assistance;
- To research and record information, compile data, compute simple arithmetic operations, and to compare numeric and alphabetical data;

- To classify information and to carry out specific problem-solving actions;
- To perform data entry tasks;
- To complete third party insurance reimbursement forms;
- To keyboard at 50 words per minute.

The course requirements include business English and composition, spelling and vocabulary, keyboarding, computer basics in programs such as WordPerfect and Lotus, information and data processing, customer service, telephone techniques, business math, medical terminology, recordkeeping, group dynamics, and professional development.

Upon completion of the program, graduates may find entry-level employment as customer service clerks and representatives, including titles such as receptionists, information clerks, postal clerks, and sales attendants. Although the competency level may be basic in some cases, these individuals may become excellent employees because of their interest in service jobs.

PERSONAL AND BEHAVIORAL QUALITIES

Hiring the right people for service jobs is crucial for success. Although the required skills and knowledge may vary, the behavior and personal characteristics of the individual are critical to the delivery of superior customer service. These qualities actually send messages to the customer, such as ''We care about you,'' ''We want to please you,'' ''You are important.'' What are some of these behavioral and personal features?

First, customer service employees need to be friendly and able to make the customer feel both welcome and comfortable: show interest; use diplomacy; be sensitive to customer's problems.

Second, employees need to have the self-esteem and maturity to deal with all kinds of customer service situations. Insecurity on the part of the employee has an impact on the relationship with the customer.

Third, employees need to possess excellent interpersonal skills so that they can communicate with the customer, respond to product inquiries, explain what can and cannot be accomplished, and follow through on problems and/or promises so that customer rapport can be created and maintained. Employees need to be able to paraphrase statements made by the customer, listen carefully, make eye contact, smile, and compliment the customer when appropriate.

Fourth, employees need to be tolerant and have a high level of self-control so that they can maintain their concern, empathy, and composure in dealing with many customers.

Desatnick discusses the behavioral characteristics that constitute a service orientation. In addition to oral communication skills and concern for others, he mentions cooperation and teamwork, problem-solving and decision-making abilities, dependability, good judgment, enthusiasm, a high energy level, flexibility, and adaptability.

Gatlin and Gatlin state that educators must go beyond simply stressing a good attitude. They need to teach the specific behavior patterns that are associated with customer satisfaction. They refer to the "four Cs" of customer service: customer orientation, conscientiousness, consistency, and courtesy. Individuals who go into customer service need to not only know these behaviors but must be consistent in using them.

Sometimes employees become involved in behavior that isn't appropriate when dealing with customers. They should refrain from complaining about the company; should not talk to other employees while waiting on a customer, argue with a customer, ignore a customer, or talk about someone else in the company when waiting on a customer. They should not respond to a customer's question with "I don't know," rather than trying to be helpful and getting the information. Employees should not just tell customers where they can find an item without leading them to the location.

In customer service, actions speak louder than words. Set an example by performing well on the job, whether you are in a managerial or non-managerial position. Talk to your customers about their needs and determine how you can help them. Michael LeBoeuf in *How to Win Customers and Keep Them for Life* refers to the Dallas-based Southland Corporation to demonstrate customer service by requiring each manager to work at least one eight-hour shift per year in a 7–Eleven Store. The company also sponsors a Neighborhood Walk program in which store managers walk through the neighborhood, knock on doors, and leave a gift packet containing a personal letter from the store manager, coupons for free beverages, and a customer comment card. These actions show that the customer comes first. Another benefit comes from the feedback on service that the store receives.

COMMUNICATION SKILLS

Communication is power. Stuart Sobel and Gary Hines in "Cray's New Focus on Customers," state that effective communications include:

- Building and maintaining positive relationships within a company and with the customer;
- Finding out what the customer expects;
- Keeping both the company and customer informed;
- Creating an awareness of services provided by the company.

Happy, motivated people are more likely to render good customer service and to treat others with respect. The three communications skills that help managers supervise their staff more effectively, according to Ken Blanchard in "Communication is the Key to Effective Management," are indicated below:

1. Be specific when giving instructions. For example, when the telephone rings, pick up no later than the second ring.
2. Build self-esteem by helping employees feel good about themselves and their actions. Compliment them on the way they handled a specific job and the positive effect that resulted.
3. Listen to what an individual is saying to fully understand the message.

Communication occurs in many forms. It may be in face-to-face discussions, writing, or telecommunications. In any one of these forms, messages are influenced by your listening skills, facial expressions, body language, and kinesthetics. Each form has a purpose.

Telephone Communication

Although many employee representatives meet face to face with their customers, a large percentage of contacts are made by telephone. Of course, it varies from business to business, depending on its operations. You should be aware of the different types of telephone communications:

Voice Communications   A term for people talking on a telephone, whether it be two individuals on a single line or eight on a teleconference setup.

Video Communications   A system by which television signals are transmitted over telephone lines so that individuals can participate in a video conference.

Facsimile Communications A system by which images of correspondence are transmitted over telephone paths.

Data Communications   A system by which information is changed into electronic signals and sent over telephone paths.

Generally, you will be successful in telephone communication if you practice the same good interpersonal skills that you use in any situation. Most help wanted ads for customer service jobs stipulate that they want applicants with "pleasant voice and phone 'personality,' " "excellent verbal and follow-up skills," and "excellent phone personality." The best approach to developing productive telephone techniques that foster good customer relationships is to plan your call. This helps you organize your ideas and focus on the purpose. Design a form that indicates the following items: person called, company (if applicable), telephone number, date and time of call, objectives, questions to ask, and action taken. Leave adequate space to record comments in each section. Be sure to discuss your business goals and reach some type of conclusion before you engage in the small talk that contributes to relationships.

When using the telephone, think of it as an opportunity to make a good impression. The first encounter is extremely important. If the customer is treated favorably, then the likelihood exists for doing business again. Use the telephone to advantage to build up the image of your company. In IBM's "It's Your Call" program as reported by Tim Ohsann in "Is Anyone There?," the following guideposts were suggested for phone calls and phone mail:

Phone Calls

- Take ownership of every call and leave a positive image of yourself and the company.
- Get information for a caller as quickly as you can and call to verify whether the customer is satisfied.
- Return calls promptly, no more than two hours later.
- Check for messages four times a day.
- Acknowledge all calls.
- Respond to callers' messages even if you don't recognize their names.
- Remember the time differences when making calls.

PhoneMail

- Keep your greeting current, brief, and friendly.
- Transfer PhoneMail calls to a phone at a desk of an individual who can answer for you or knows where you can be reached.
- PhoneMail is not to be used for screening calls.

Reprinted by permission from *Think* Magazine, Copyright 1990, International Business Machines Corporation.

Telecommunications has created many jobs in industry. Some salespeople, in particular, perform the major part of their work over the telephone. Their titles may be telephone order clerks or telephone solicitors.

TELEMARKETING

The telephone has been used as a marketing tool for a long time; however, in more recent years, companies see the advantages of this technique, now known as *telemarketing*. AT&T in "Making Advertising Pay Off" defines telemarketing as a "planned combination of trained staff, telecommunications, and management information systems to provide customer services, take orders, or proactively sell your products or services."

Originally, "cold calling" was the process used where names were just picked at random. This procedure is now being replaced by "target marketing," which selects a particular clientele. Telemarketing is handled by a special department within a firm or an agency. It may be used with other forms of communications, such as direct mail or advertising. Telemarketing is used by both large and small companies.

Telemarketing is a growth area for career opportunities. It is used for a variety of activities that include selling, market research, customer service, building customer relationships, response to inquiries, and follow-up goodwill calls. Some position titles are telephone customer service representatives, market support representatives, order processing representatives, residential service representatives, commercial service representatives, customer support representatives, telemarketing center manager, and telemarketing communicators. The one factor that each of these positions has in common is the need for good communication and interpersonal skills. The heart of telemarketing is customer interaction.

Written Communications

When you correspond in writing to a customer, use the "you" approach and his/her name. For example, say, "You will receive a . . . on your next purchase" instead of "We will see what we can do . . ." This shows that you are interested in your customers and want to satisfy their needs. Also, use action words and, above all, be honest. Honesty does not preclude trying to be helpful, even though you can't promise results. Write in nontechnical, easy-to-understand language that the customer can understand. Be concise and to the point. If possible, try to use words that match those used by the customer.

Other Communications Skills

Body language   Facial expressions and body language communicate feelings, attitudes, and ideas. A nod can mean ''I understand.'' A smile says ''I enjoy working with you.'' Keeping your arms folded below your chest could indicate a distant attitude and that you aren't interested. If you enter a store or an office and nobody greets you or asks how he or she can help you, the message you get is that nobody cares. Use your body language to try to mirror the customer at his or her level. For example, if a customer appears very enthusiastic and excited about a product, try to appear the same.

Kinesthetics   Customers like the sensation of movement and touch. They prefer handling merchandise and the personal contact that comes with a handshake. If you can sense this feeling about your customer, then you could appropriately use this style of communication.

Listening

Statistics show that listening is approximately 45 percent of our communicating behavior. To understand what the customer is or is not saying and to understand feelings, desires, and concerns, you need to listen and not interrupt. By listening attentively to your customers, you are showing them that you care. If you can determine the type of person the customer is, then you can tailor your own communications. To make customers comfortable, listen to the level of voice, pitch, and pace of customer.

Effective listening provides the opportunity to gather information and ideas from your customers. You can learn about a customer's needs, priorities, and demands; an individual's productivity; problems encountered; and resources needed to complete a task. Make a real effort to listen to your customers as you conduct your daily activities. Listening is vital in personal, face-to-face conversations. It is equally important as you interact with others, whether it be in the supermarket, bank, or even on the street; in direct contact at meetings, conferences, or community gatherings; by customer hotlines that have toll-free numbers for customer service; through comments and complaints; or by research conducted through surveys, both formal and informal.

Blanchard says that listening to employees "makes them feel understood and supported, which encourages them to do better work. Good listening skills also strengthen the relationship between a manager and employee."

The importance of listening is demonstrated in Tom Peters statement: "Listening to customers *must* become everyone's business. With most competitors moving ever faster, the race will go to those who listen (and respond) most intently."

COMPANY TRAINING PROGRAMS

Training is a term that describes a variety of activities frequently used in conjunction with human resource development (HRD). It is defined in the American Society of Training and Development's (ASTD) *Reference Guide to Professional Training Roles and Competencies* as "organized learning experiences sponsored by an employer and designed and/or conducted for the purpose of improving work performance.'' It is considered an investment in the human resources of the company, which should ultimately lead to excellent customer service.

Training in customer service makes a difference. Desatnick believes that ''people will do the right things and do things right, if they are properly trained to do so.'' Training should be focused, constant, and intensive. Employees need technical training to execute job responsibilities which will meet their customers' needs. Equally important are the behavioral skills that are so vital to all employees who have contact with customers. The training might be formal or informal.

In a formal training program, the course name, meeting dates, and time allocation are specified. Frequently, a company uses independent study in which computer-based training (CBT) and videos are used. The individual advances at his or her own rate. Informally, a new employee might receive on-the-job training by a peer or by a supervisor. At times, a consultant might be called in for a special presentation, such as a demonstration on how to calm irate customers, what to listen for when handling complaints, and how to resolve conflict.

Should all employees be required to take the same courses? Not necessarily! First, the performance of specific responsibilities varies with the position. Front-line employees may require certain courses that differ from office staff and managers. Second, people are different and have varying levels of expertise. They need to see the value of a course and understand how it will improve their personal development. Individuals who perceive this need will be motivated to study and learn. The education that all service workers should obtain, however, focuses on interpersonal skills when dealing with customers and other employees.

At Cray's Research, Sobel and Hines report that training is essential to an employee development system. This training will improve an individual's knowledge, skills, and attitudes in the four key areas that affect customer service and satisfaction. These areas include:

- the company
- job functions
- supporting and working with co-workers
- providing customer service/meeting the customer's needs

A special program on Product Familiarization and Understanding Cray Business was designed to inform employees about the company so that they can answer customer questions and be prepared to promote a product.

Another interesting, unique program sponsored by Cray Research is Managing Customer Relations, a structured meeting of everyone involved with a particular account. Action planning sessions are held which include customers as well as managers, salespersons, and all account service personnel. These sessions provide feedback from a customer's perspective and the action taken relates to customer satisfaction.

Customer participation, as used by Cray, is a fairly new concept that some companies are using to determine what customers want, to find ways of providing better service, and to expose salespeople to customer concerns. These meetings are called *focus groups*. Originally, such meetings were conducted by professional facilitators from marketing research firms. Selected customers were solicited to attend for a fee.

For example, several years ago, the author was invited by such a research firm on behalf of a publisher, in order to get feedback on office practice textbooks. Six users of textbooks in this area were present; dialogue and responses to questions were recorded; and evaluation and results were reported back to the client. Nowadays the format is changing, and companies do their own planning, hosting, evaluation, and follow-up. Questions are directed to the customer; weaknesses in operational processes and policies are determined; training needs are assessed. Salespeople begin to understand the real world, and they can ask questions that will help them perform better. Stronger relationships are developed with customers.

A Citicorp study of seventeen role model companies, according to Desatnick, indicated that all of their training programs focused on three areas: job-related skills, positive attitudes toward customers and co-workers, and overall company knowledge.

A study by Learning International of 150 employees in organizations striving for service excellence, as summarized in *Lessons From Top Service Providers,* 1991, indicates that these companies have a philosophical commitment to superior service. One method to empower their customer service providers is by expanding their roles and capabilities. Employees are coached and trained "to understand and meet or exceed customer service expectations." Their educational programs consist of extensive orientation; training in key skills, knowledge, and attitudes required for the position; reinforcement training as well as study in other functional areas; career development, counseling, and coaching; and a performance review system connected to goals for improvement. The participating organizations in this study believe these development tactics benefit the company in several ways: reinforcing critical competencies; motivating and retaining customer service employees; alleviating stress; keeping individuals challenged; leading to greater job satisfaction; and increasing company loyalty.

In addition to the usual courses in problem solving, interpersonal communications, and listening, these organizations add subjects that were once reserved exclusively for management: stress management, public speaking, and handling specific customer situations or populations. The ultimate aim is to develop front-line people into true professionals. A developmental plan is designed for each employee, performance is tracked, and feedback is given. Managers and supervisors play an integral part in motivating and challenging the employee.

Some training suggestions for customer service employees are as follows:

- Plan personnel development. Identify competencies to be studied and establish a schedule for training and follow-up.
- Give performance feedback readily; assign senior representatives the responsibility of giving help when needed; provide managers with the coaching skills they need to improve staff performance.
- Management must make the time to train customer service representatives and to answer their questions so that they can respond knowledgeably to customers' questions.
- Offer ''cross training'' to the firm's service professionals; be sure that they understand the company's philosophy, culture, and operations.

Another source of training that can enhance the knowledge and skills of service workers is the conferences and seminars sponsored by professional organizations, such as the AFSM International. Some of the topics discussed at the 1991 World Conference and Exhibition in San Francisco, California, were ''Managing Customer Perception,'' ''The Future of Telecommunications,'' ''The Service Marketplace in 1995,'' and ''Value Added Services—A Case Study.''

Jack Gordon in "Where The Training Goes" discusses the job categories of people employed in organizations with over 100 employees: who receives formal instruction, the subjects taught, and the delivery of training. Figure 19 displays a ranking of "training intensity" for five job classifications. Forty-five percent of the organizations provide training for customer service people, compared to 40.4 percent for salespeople. Most organizations offer training for professionals, 59.6 percent; first-line supervisors, 73.3 percent; and middle managers, 75.9 percent. It is enlightening to know that the number of hours allocated to training for customer service workers has risen for the past two years. Also interesting to note is that the mean number of customer service people trained, 91.6 percent, surpassed the other categories.

Figure 20 shows the percentage of organizations that offered training in general topic areas during 1990. Over 70 percent provided training in customer relations/services, and over 45 percent in customer education.

Most of the training was given by in-house personnel and a smaller percentage by outside consultants and suppliers that may have included universities. The three methods used most

Figure 19

WHO GETS THE TRAINING

Job Category	% of Organizations	Mean No. of Individuals
Salespeople	40.4	65.1
Professionals	59.6	68.1
First-Line Supervisors	73.3	38.4
Middle Managers	75.9	25.4
Customer Service People	45.0	91.6

SOURCE: Reprinted with permission from the October, 1990 issue of TRAINING Magazine, Copyright 1990, Lakewood Publications, Inc., Minneapolis, MN, (612) 333-0471. All rights reserved.

Figure 20

GENERAL TYPES OF TRAINING

Type of Training	% of Organizations
Management Skills/Development	86.2
Technical Skills/Knowledge	83.0
Supervisory Skills	82.4
Communication Skills	78.2
Customer Relations/Services	70.8
Customer Education	45.2

SOURCE: Reprinted with permission from the October, 1990 issue of TRAINING Magazine, Copyright 1990, Lakewood Publications, Inc., Minneapolis, MN, (612) 333-0471. All rights reserved.

frequently to deliver the instruction were videotapes, 88.7 percent; lectures, 84.1 percent; and one-on-one instruction, 72.2 percent.

To determine trends, respondents were asked the following question: "In your opinion, what general topic or trend will present the most critical challenge to your organization's training and development function over the next two to five years?" The two topics that took second and third place were customer service at 14.9 percent and quality improvement at 14.4 percent, respectively. See Figure 21 for the top five challenges for human resource departments. In organizations with 500 to 999 employees, quality improvement leads the list (20 percent).

Other significant data on training challenges by industrial categories are reflected in Figure 22. The top four types of organizations that offered training in customer relations/services were finance/insurance/banking institutions, 92.9 percent; wholesale/retail trade, 79 percent; transportation/communications/utilities, 74.9 percent; and manufacturing 67.3 percent.

Figure 21

TRAINING AND DEVELOPMENT CHALLENGES

Topic	*% of Organizations*
Technological Change	16.2
Customer Service	14.9
Quality Improvement	14.4
Corportate Culture	9.1
New Market Strategies Organizational Missions	8.1

CANADIAN PERSPECTIVE ON TRAINING

To be competitive in today's global marketplace, training and education should be given top priority by Canadian businesses. These programs, union leaders agree, should be subsidized by employers. A survey of 119 business leaders and 72 union leaders by Canada's Labor Market and Productivity Center (CLMPC) revealed the following findings:

- Education and training are more important than lower interest rates, a lower government deficit, or increased spending for research and development, according to more than one-third of the responding businesspeople and nearly 40 percent of the union leaders.
- Both employers and unions should be directly involved in the training of employees.
- Employers are responsible for training and retraining, as well as funding.
- Labor leaders support the concept of a national training tax on corporations. More than 75 percent of the business leaders oppose such a tax.

Figure 22

GENERAL TYPES OF TRAINING BY INDUSTRY

Type of Training	A	B	C	D
Management Skills/Development	82.9	83.7	81.9	92.0
Technical Skills/Knowledge	82.8	87.6	69.3	89.2
Supervisory Skills	81.6	84.0	74.4	92.7
Communication Skills	73.4	79.7	62.8	90.5
Customer Relations/Services	67.3	74.9	79.0	92.9
Customer Education	56.8	46.8	46.4	48.8

Legend: A – Manufacturing

B – Transportation/Communications/Utilities

C – Wholesale/Retail Trade

D – Finance/Insurance/Banking

SOURCE: Reprinted with permission from the October, 1990 issue of TRAINING Magazine, Copyright 1990, Lakewood Publications, Inc., Minneapolis, MN, (612) 333-0471. All rights reserved.

- Business leaders value international competitiveness essential to maintaining a high standard of living, in contrast to union leaders who don't place the same importance on it.
- Low productivity, high training costs, poor quality control, and difficult recruitment are attributed to inadequate workers' reading, writing, and mathematical skills, according to one-third of the business leaders and one-half of the labor leaders.
- Generally, respondents were unhappy with current training programs.

• Inadequate facilities for training and low interest in training by many employers were cited as obstacles to educational programs.

From all of the previous discussion on training in both the United States and Canada, it is obvious that more attention and greater emphasis is being placed on company programs that contribute to the improvement of quality of work which affect both the organization and customer in terms of productivity and service.

Other Views from Canada

A reading of the literature supports the view that customer service in Canada is following the same track that exists in the United States.

Jim Clemmer in "The Service/Quality Revolution: An Opportunity for Public Sector Renewal," which appeared in the 1990–91 issue of *Optimum*, a Canadian periodical, quoted Alexander Graham Bell:

> When one door closes, another opens, but we often long
> so regretfully upon the closed door that we do not see the
> one which has opened for us.

Immediately following, Clemmer refers to the recession of the early '80s as a major turning point in the history of Canadian Xerox, Ford, AMP of Canada, B.C. Tel, Motorola, Reimer Express, and a host of other strong corporations. This major crisis of the '80s taught these organizations painful lessons of "doing more with less." They and their personnel continued to operate with a lot less, but surprisingly saw customer satisfaction, product quality, employee morale, and productivity continue to climb.

Many North American organizations have experienced that morale strengthens and costs decline when levels of customer service rise and the quality of the work processes are improved. However, this cannot be achieved overnight. Clemmer believes that success occurs from pulling together four broad areas, which need to act as a road map for direction:

1. Values which include commitment, listening to internal and external customers, education, and hiring;
2. Skills which include personal, coaching, team effort;
3. Alignment which includes systems and processes, rewards and recognition, standards and measures, and marketing strategies;
4. Deployment which refers to the infrastructure, planning and reporting, and assigned responsibilities.

Many of Canada's governments and institutions are experiencing their own form of recession. Federal government managers need to emulate service/quality strategies used by the private sector to improve productivity, customer satisfaction, and employee morale.

David Hillary, president of Hillary's Cleaners, states in "Our Quality is Really Job One" that "Our customers are our bread and butter." He interviews every prospective employee and when hired gives them a tour of the store and introduces them to the staff. They receive an identification tag and are told about the incentive plans and bonuses. Hillary believes in a harmonious workplace, good working conditions, and investments in technology.

David A. Bratton in "Organization Challenges of the 1990s: Leadership, Service, Culture, and Morale" indicated that 70 percent of all jobs in Canada are in the service sector. He believes that strategies for exercising leadership, providing excellent service, changing the culture, and assessing the impact of changes on employee morale are equally as important as marketing and financial strategies.

Bratton continued that the four challenges of the 1990s facing industry are as follows: 1) to develop visionary leaders capable of really leading, not just managing; 2) to view service as a major strategy; 3) to build and maintain strong cultures or values in organizations; and 4) to insure that employees see opportunities in customer service and actively cooperate with management.

". . . efforts at improving customer service aren't focused only on frontline personnel that deal with customers every day," states David Evans in "The Myth of Customer Service," in the March 1991 issue of *Canadian Business*. It needs to become an integral goal of the entire organization and a commitment from management; it might entail restructuring of the organization; shortening the distance to the customer; and reclassifying job functions according to customers' priorities. A full commitment to superior customer service requires substantial investments in employee training, incentives, infrastructure, communications, and marketing.

From the public sector, Ronald S. Clark states in "Quality Public Service: The Ottawa-Carleton Experience" that "Complacency and a misguided sense of security that may come with the delivery of essential public services have no place in an organization dedicated to recognizing the primacy of our customers—the municipal taxpayers." At the Regional Municipality of Ottawa-Carleton (RMOC) where Clark is chief administrative officer, budgets are not cut for staff training and development. Resources are provided to allow employees to grow and flourish. RMOC is committed to its personnel, for people who work in the organization cannot provide quality customer service if they aren't treated with care.

In essence, all of the previous views express the same thought: Organizations that are committed to quality service will have a greater opportunity for survival even during difficult economic times if they can retain their customers' loyalty.

Quality-Control Analysts. Apparently this is a job title used in Canada for someone who has responsibilities of controlling quality of processes and products. In another company, this same position might be titled technician or perhaps engineer in still another firm. Some duties of the position include the following:

- Making statistical analyses of production and services information affecting operations of industrial establishments;
- Participating in the production sales and marketing of a product;
- Leading efforts to implement total quality management by improving process quality within companies.

The general requirements for such a position are an educational degree in quality technology, management, or science from a college, university, or technical school with satisfactory endorsement by the American Society for Quality Control, Canadian Chapters.

ASQC certification can be achieved by meeting the criteria of education and work experience and a written examination.

Comparable Worth Policy. This policy has been part of a steady evolution of equal pay policies in Canada. Employers with more than ten workers must assess jobs in which at least 60 percent of the employees are women. Evaluation of similarities is based on skill, effort, responsibilities, and working conditions. Comparable worth is seen ''as a form of redress that does not require women to leave the female-dominated, low-wage job ghettos to improve their economic position.''

CHAPTER 7

ADVANCEMENT OPPORTUNITIES IN CUSTOMER SERVICE POSITIONS

Are you the kind of person who wants to be hired into a dead-end job? If you are a career-oriented individual, then the answer would be "No!" Undoubtedly, you have set goals for yourself. To achieve these goals, you need to plan your strategies and work at them until you believe you qualify for a promotion. You must not only perform the responsibilities of your present job with great success, but you need to be a customer-oriented person—innovative, articulate, able to think like the customer, able to keep the mission of the firm in mind when handling customers, do more than is required of you, and be willing to become involved in special projects. In many organizations, promotions are made from within the ranks, according to Joseph Trpik of the *AFSM International*. Many service executives who were hired at an entry-level job and who demonstrated good customer skills were promoted from level to level until they reached the top. Each time they advanced, they were managing people with the same skills in which they were proficient.

While working at the entry-level position, you gain experience—experience which either confirms your expectations of the job or is a disappointment. If you believe you have found the career for you, then to advance in the company you need to assess your abilities and continue to improve and expand them. Get to know your company—its product, its structure, and its philosophy. This information will give you the background you need to have so that you can determine which strengths you need to develop. Advancement generally means a new title, more challenges, greater responsibility, more complex work, more decision making, and even the opportunity to supervise others.

Advancement just doesn't happen. You plan for it and work at it. Maximize all work experiences; pursue your education either through continuing education courses, seminars, or workshops; join professional organizations and take an active role; read the professional literature and network with the individuals you meet at meetings and social gatherings. Learn about the different kinds of customer service positions in the firm where you are employed and in other industries. From these associations, you gain a broad perspective of the field. A professional affiliation is motivational and frequently encourages you to engage in activities for professional growth, such as the development of newer skills and knowledge.

In Chapter 3, you read about the different types and levels of positions in customer service, including some of the basic duties of the job. In Chapter 5, titles at advanced levels that were used within specific companies were identified. In this chapter, you will learn more about the personal qualities needed for a career in customer service and the professional organizations that are supporting customer services as a profession.

PERSONAL POWER

Since customer service employees are found in practically all industries and professions, the responsibilities are diversified, depending on the nature of the firm, the department in which you are employed, and the mission of the organization. The single most important focus of all these companies is the need for customer service, which is the bottom line for survival and success. Many companies have also installed new automated equipment and have devised sophisticated systems to render better service; however, without the right mix of employees who have the appropriate personal attributes, at both subordinate and managerial levels, the total mission of the company will not be achieved.

Although a quality product is still essential, in of itself it will not acquire and retain a customer. It is the employee who talks to customers and who satisfies them. It is this employee who will ultimately affect company profits through customer retention and loyalty. Building positive relationships with customers and effectiveness in handling individual problems are attributable to personal power of the customer service employee. What are some of the attributes these employees should demonstrate?

- like people and be happy with their own work;
- care about the customers and interact with them in a manner that shows concern and respect;
- strive to be helpful;
- empathize with the customers and try to see things from their point of view;
- display honesty and ethical behavior;
- be perceptive and tactful;
- maintain patience even under stressful situations;

- use words and phrases that are understood by customer;
- listen actively to customer;
- demonstrate a mental alertness;
- exercise good judgment in giving information to customer;
- know when to modify company procedures to satisfy a customer (for example, crediting a customer account to maintain loyalty);
- demonstrate leadership skills—inspire others, serve as role model, solve problems, involve others in carrying out projects, encourage team spirit, recognize excellent performance, motivate employees to be creative and to perform at a high level, share knowledge, and maintain morale;
- maintain a professional image;
- display loyalty to company.

PROFESSIONAL ORGANIZATIONS

Joining a professional organization is beneficial to both the employee and to the employer—the employee in terms of professional growth; the employer in terms of visibility and support given to the discipline it represents. For the member, it is one way of keeping abreast of changes in the field, the trends, and even the competition. It is an excellent method for becoming acquainted with other individuals in the field and is a resource for gathering information and for developing ideas. In addition, you can strengthen your credentials. By becoming active after you join the group, you will have an opportunity to develop your communication and leadership skills and broaden your knowledge base.

Companies frequently pay membership dues for their employees who join the organization and might even reimburse them for costs incurred when attending meetings and conferences.

Several organizations devoted to the field of customer service about which you should become knowledgeable are detailed below.

The International Customer Service Association (ICSA). Located at 401 North Michigan Avenue, Chicago, IL 60611, the ICSA was founded in 1981 for customer service management professionals. They have a membership of 3,100 people in 39 chapters, including one in Toronto. The local chapters promote customer service interaction, leadership, and professionalism. It also gives members the opportunity to network and share experiences.

The mission of ICSA was redefined in 1990 and reads: ''to develop the theory and understanding of the total quality service process, advance the art and science of managing that process, and encourage professional dialogue to the achievement, of customer satisfaction.'' Through a diversity of programs and activities, the value of customer service is promoted and enhanced. Some of their special projects include the following:

- an annual Customer Service Week that focuses on the importance of the customer and the customer service profession (this week has already been proclaimed by 27 states in the U.S.);
- a Quality Service Award which recognizes employees at all levels and which provides cash awards and incentives;
- an Award of Excellence given to two companies each year who best display a corporate culture that is committed to quality customer service at all levels of the organization;
- conferences, workshops, and continuing education programs;

- a data bank of customer service professionals with expertise in specific customer service-related topics, which is shared with ICSA members;
- promoting corporate executive understanding of customer service as a marketing force in improving customer satisfaction and corporate profits;
- cooperation with schools, colleges, and universities in curriculum development for customer service programs;

The organization sponsors an annual convention, publishes an annual membership directory and a bimonthly newsletter which reports on customer service innovations and practices implemented by ICSA members. The Education and Research Committee undertakes special projects when appropriate, such as surveys for updating information on the customer service profession. The organization also sponsors a professional certification program for qualified customer service professionals. You will read more about this program in the next section, *Certification Programs*.

The ICSA has two different categories of membership: regular members for management professionals working in the customer service function and affiliate members who support the customer service profession and include individuals such as trainers, educators, suppliers, consultants, etc.

The Association for Services Management International (AFSMI) Located at 1342 Colonial Boulevard, Suite 25, Fort Myers, Florida, AFSMI is another organization dedicated to field service as a professional discipline. It was founded in 1976, has 43 local chapters, and 6,000 members. The different categories of membership are the following: 1) professional member for individuals who are directly involved in the day-to-day management of a high technology service business; 2) associate member for those persons who are interested in supporting the industry and the goals of the Association; 3) retired associate member who wants to continue affiliation; and 4) student associate member who is interested in growing into the management ranks in the high technology services industry.

The AFSMI sponsors a diversity of training seminars and workshops, which may be tailored to the individual needs of an organization. At their annual conferences, industry leaders conduct each seminar. The 18th AFSMI World Conference and Exhibition, held in San Francisco, California, featured topics such as ''Changing Customer Dissatisfaction to Customer Satisfaction,'' ''Managing Customer Perception,'' and ''The Service Marketplace in 1995.'' A College Degree Program is also one of the organization's special projects to meet the varying membership educational needs. An independent study program designed for management growth has been developed with Syracuse University. Upon fulfilling all of the requirements, the individual earns a BS degree in Business Administration.

Other projects the AFSMI sponsors are a *Services/Support Personnel Compensation Survey,* a member inquiry service, a record of case histories, a file of course programs and outlines, and an awards program. The organization also publishes *The Professional Journal* monthly. It is a comprehensive publication and includes book reviews of literature related to the field.

This organization has played a major role in defining the industry. As indicated in their literature, research conducted by the association shows that the common thread in all services/support advancements are the management skills and special disciplines required. These span general management, managing personnel, technical training, repair centers, customer support centers, and service marketing.

CERTIFICATION PROGRAM

The ICSA has a certification program which was developed to certify and publicly recognize qualified customer service executives and professionals. The objectives of the program are to inspire customer service personnel to strive for higher levels of professional improvement, to increase standards, and to identify individuals who possess the knowledge and skill of a professional in their career field.

To be eligible for certification, you need at least three years of experience in customer service; and you must complete a comprehensive certification application. Certification is based on a point system allocated to local chapter participation; international association participation; classes, seminars, and degree programs completed; and an essay on one of the following subjects:

1. the most significant contribution you personally have made to the profession of customer service,
2. how your company uses customer service as an integral part of corporate strategy,
3. your ideas on what constitutes effective customer service training and the training programs you have developed.

All information must be verified with supporting data. Individuals who are certified may use the designation CCSP after their names. Those persons who wish to be certified as a customer service executive have to accumulate more points and write a lengthier essay. CCSE is the designation for this level.

NETWORKING

Building relationships with others is helpful to you in achieving your goals. A group of individuals with whom you communicate, share ideas, exchange career information, give leads to jobs, and lend moral support is known as a *network*. A network is similar to a team effort in which people cooperate with each other so that an individual becomes more knowledgeable and succeeds in accomplishing a task or reaching a goal—such as finding a job in a particular area or industry that they may not have been able to reach independently. The people you meet through memberships in associations and those with whom you begin to interact gradually become a professional resource network that is invaluable in your career. As a member of a network of individuals who are interested in the same career field as you, you always have a potential source of information, advice, and support. Networking is the vehicle through which you establish business contacts, meet people from every aspect of the service industry, and keep current on changing trends in industry.

CHAPTER 8

THE JOB SEARCH

The job market is beset with layoffs that are occurring at an alarming rate. Corporations such as Colgate-Palmolive Co., PepsiCo Inc., and Time Warner Inc. have begun to cut costs and to downsize. Another massive elimination of 2,500 white collar jobs occurred at Xerox. These are some of our most important major corporations. On the brighter side, customer service as a career has been less affected. Where the layoffs occurred at Xerox is probably indicative of the trend in industry: The reductions at Xerox came from their document-processing business. According to Paul A. Allaire, the company's chairman and chief executive, the reductions are part of ''our ongoing process to create a more efficient, flatter, customer-responsive organization.'' That statement portends well for individuals who have chosen customer service as the career they wish to pursue.

HOW DO I BEGIN?

The job search is a time-consuming task that may create anxiety. As you begin to plan your strategies for the search, try to use this period as a learning opportunity. You will begin to gain confidence and take control of your actions. First you must ask yourself several questions so that you can focus in on very specific areas:

1. What specifically do I want to do?
2. Do I have the skills and knowledge for this area? What are my strengths, likes, and dislikes?
3. Am I a people person?
4. Am I flexible or rigid in my ideas?
5. Do I prefer a small or a large firm?
6. What should I have in my portfolio?
7. How do I get an interview?

Assuming that you want to pursue a career in customer service, then relate everything else you do in your job search to this employment area.

Strengths, likes, and dislikes inventory. Take stock of yourself to determine what skills and knowledge you possess—those skills in which you excel and those areas of study and play that were most enjoyable. Design a three-column Inventory Form that indicates your strengths, likes, and dislikes in which to write your response (See Figure 23). As you begin to take a critical look at yourself, think back to the time when you enjoyed running errands, were a scout leader, were on a school committee, won a keyboarding contest, took computer courses using a specific software program such as WordPerfect 5.1, and learned basic accounting. Did you find that you were generally successful in doing those things you liked best?

Personal traits inventory. Think about your activities in the past, both at school and with your friends, and then evaluate yourself as to the type of person you are—someone who likes being with other people or working with people, a stickler for rules or willing to bend, a team player, friendly, analytical.

Figure 23

STRENGTHS, LIKES, AND DISLIKES INVENTORY

Strengths	Likes	Dislikes

After the above two inventories have been completed, review the items and select those qualities that are necessary for a customer service entry-level position. Then write a one- or two-sentence paragraph identifying those skills and personal qualities that are essential in dealing with customers. This would be a good statement to use when you ''sell'' yourself during an interview.

JOB LOCATION, SIZE OF FIRM, TYPE OF INDUSTRY

You have a choice of working either in a suburban community or in the city, now that many office buildings and Industrial Parks have been constructed in the suburbs. In a suburban area, travel time and expenses are reduced, parking facilities are available, the areas are landscaped and surroundings quiet. The cities have lots of activity and crowds, shopping is close by, salaries are generally higher, cultural activities are available, greater emphasis is placed on dress, and expenses are greater. In what kind of environment would you be happier?

You must also consider size of firm and where your strengths will be most visible. If you like diversity in responsibility, then a small firm might be a wise choice for you. Usually, fewer people are employed, the atmosphere is informal, you have greater freedom in rearranging work schedules, and supervision is minimal. In terms of advancement, it is limited. In a large firm, you may specialize in a particular area; policies and procedures are formalized; vertical or lateral advancement is possible; company benefits are available, such as training programs, company-subsidized cafeterias, tuition reimbursement plans, and day care centers.

The type of industry is another consideration. For example, if you enjoy music, you might prefer working in a firm that sells music and instruments. If you enjoy art, a museum shop or an art gallery might be a possibility. Although this might seem like the best route to take, don't sell yourself by industry. Market yourself by your skills and profession. These are your assets. Then search for employment where your experiences will contribute to your professional growth. Ask yourself the following questions before you take the job:

1. Will the knowledge I gain on this job add to my expertise for my career goal?
2. Is the company progressive and current?
3. Will my existing knowledge and skills be used in this position?
4. Is the company's philosophy supportive of the assignment offered to me?
5. What is the person like who will be my supervisor? sincere? receptive to new ideas? flexible?

WHERE DO YOU FIND JOB LEADS?

You can search for a position in a variety of ways. Following is a list of suggestions:

Network with your friends, acquaintances, and relatives. Discuss with them the kind of position you are seeking and ask them to remember you when they know of a job that is available. Frequently, they, too, might hear about an opening from a friend of theirs. This is probably one of the best job-getting techniques.

Instructors and school placement offices receive calls from businesses about job openings. Talk to your instructor about your career goals and file your portfolio with the placement office. The portfolio should include recommendations from instructors, a resume, and other credentials.

Computerized job banks, which occasionally require a student listing fee, are another source. Check with your placement office for names of reputable commercial job data banks.

Yellow Pages of the telephone directory can be used to make ''cold calls'' to personnel departments. Your call might reach the company at a very opportune time.

Walk in to a personnel department where you will be given an application to complete.

Job fairs are held by colleges. Recruiters distribute information about their companies, discuss opportunities, and may interview job seekers.

CLASSIFIED ADS IN NEWSPAPERS AND PROFESSIONAL MAGAZINES

Ads list job openings under various categories. Think about the various classifications under which the type of job you are looking for might appear. Read these ads regularly. You will gain insight as to where the jobs are, the salaries offered, and the skill requirements. Familiarize yourself with the four types of ads:

1. the open ad, which gives you a company name and address;
2. the blind ad which indicates a box or telephone number only so that they can eliminate unqualified applicants;
3. high-powered ads that attract attention by exciting descriptions, while qualifications required of job seekers aren't mentioned; and
4. agency ads, both public and private, which do not indicate name of employer.

You do not pay a fee to a public employment agency. The state employment agencies are linked to a network by the U.S. Employment Service. Private employment agencies charge a fee; however, this is usually paid by the employer. Be cautious when using these private agencies. Sometimes they advertise a job that is not available when you get to their place of business. Register with several agencies that specialize in your field of work. Be prepared to go through a preliminary screening process, testing, and an interview.

For every job prospect, keep a record of the source on a 3 1/2″ x 5″ index card. Include type of position, company name, address, contact person, and telephone number. On the reverse side, indicate the action you took, the date, and the results.

Conduct an active job search. Do not wait for things to happen!

MAKING YOUR RESUME WORK FOR YOU

Your resume is the tool that might get you the interview. It is a vital part of the job search. It helps sell your qualifications as a job candidate to the employer, and it prepares you for the interview. Be careful in enumerating skills and accomplishments. Your resume should be a reflection of you and should support the goals you have set for yourself. Begin to develop your resume by gathering information about yourself, your education, your work experience, and special interests and talents. Be specific. For example, under education, indicate the school, city and state, degree earned, date, major area of concentration, related courses, and skills (including languages). Under work experience, indicate firm name, address, department, supervisor, and responsibilities of the job.

After you have gathered the necessary information, you are ready to develop the resume. A sample resume for an individual interested in customer service is shown in Figure 24. Keep the following in mind:

Career Objective. Focus in on a specific type of position and, if you wish, include your ultimate goal: "To work as a customer service representative, using the skills that I have mastered in my school and at work. My ultimate goal is to become a supervisor and achieve certification in the field."

Education. If you have a college degree, you need not include your high school background. Give complete information, as detailed above.

Work Experience. This section will be read carefully by your prospective employer to determine if your past work experience relates to the company's needs. Use reverse chronological order. Highlight significant data and use action verbs to describe your duties, such as "maintained" and "resolved."

Special Interests and Talents. Mention every position that you held, whether it was at college or in community organizations, that would show leadership ability and good interpersonal skills.

References. These do not have to be included in the resume. However, when you do select individuals as references, select employers, supervisors, and instructors who can speak with authority about your personal qualifications and skills. Do not use friends or relatives as references. Be sure to ask for permission to use an individual's name for reference.

There are several acceptable styles. You may use the model resume in Figure 24 as you develop your own.

THE INTERVIEW MAKES A DIFFERENCE

The job interview is one of the final steps in getting hired. In this face-to-face meeting with either a personnel director, supervisor, or employer, you have to sell yourself as the person for the job. During the interview, the interviewer will assess your qualifications, including your behavior and appearance. You, at the same time, will have an opportunity to learn more about the company and the job responsibilities. You can then decide if the position meets your career goals.

Follow these guidelines as you prepare for the interview. In your portfolio, be sure to have your resume and other relevant documents. Research the company, including its products and services; anticipate growth of company; gather information on its reputation for employee-employer relations; anticipate questions that might be asked during the interview; and think about the ways in which you can make a contribution to the operations of the company.

When you enter the room where the interview will take place, remember to give the interviewer a strong handshake and wait to be invited to be seated. Try to be in control of yourself and

Figure 24

Robert White
16 Mallard Drive
Rochester, NY 14622-1512
(401) 654-9324

CAREER OBJECTIVE

To work as a customer service representative, using the skills that I have mastered at school and at work. My ultimate goal is to become a supervisor and achieve certification in the field.

EDUCATION

Syracuse University   B.S.Degree
610 East Lafayette Street
Syracuse, NY 13244-6020

FIELD OF STUDY

Business Administration

RELATED COURSES

Management and Society
Organizational Behavior
Marketing Analysis
Marketing Strategy
Marketing Planning and Control

SKILLS

Oral and written
    communications
Interpersonal skills
Conversational fluency in
    Spanish and French
IBM Personal Computer
Software programs:
    WordPerfect 5.1, Lotus
    1-2-3, and DBase III +

AWARDS AND HONORS

Dean's List each semester

WORK EXPERIENCE

Spring 1990 – present

Marshall Brothers
101 Baker Boulevard
Syracuse, NY 13209-1902

Sales Associate
Duties: Assist customers in selection and purchase of merchandise; maintain control over large inventory; resolve customer complaints

REFERENCES

Furnished on request

relaxed. Displaying self-confidence is a factor that is evaluated. Some typical questions that you might be asked follow:

- ''Tell me about yourself.'' Briefly, you might mention your educational background and related work experience, leading into the reason you are the right candidate for the job.
- ''How would you describe yourself?'' Highlight those factors that are required of personnel who deal with customers.
- ''Why did you select our company?'' This is the opportunity to use the information you gathered from your research.
- ''What are your major strengths?'' Include personal traits such as enthusiasm, maturity, assertiveness, and sensitivity to other people's feelings.
- ''What are your weaknesses?'' Turn your weaknesses into a positive statement when you respond. For example, you might indicate that at times it appears you are impatient, but you like to get your work out on schedule.
- ''What are your most important accomplishments?'' This could be the design of a new form for purchases or a new training procedure.
- ''How would you work with or accept a supervisor from a cultural background that is different from yours?'' You might indicate that you would try to learn more about that particular culture, including some of its norms and values.
- ''Would you like to ask a question of me?'' This might be the time to ask the interviewer what is expected of you, how performance evaluations are given, and what is the basis for promotions.

For customer service positions, three other approaches may be used for conducting interviews: 1) over the telephone to determine if the interviewee is the right person for a position that involves a lot of telephone contact; 2) role playing where the interviewee takes the part of the customer to determine interactions; and 3) simulations in which the job candidate is placed in a situation that is comparable to the actual job. This helps the interviewer to observe the applicant under stressful situations.

WHEN THE INTERVIEW IS OVER

After the interview is over, summarize briefly why you would be the right candidate for the job. Thank the interviewer by name for seeing you. You might ask when a decision will be made and suggest that you will call on a specific day to find out if the position has been filled.

Each interview should be a learning experience which gives you more information for the next one. Think positively about your qualifications and pursue your job search with self-confidence.

Appendix

BIBLIOGRAPHY

Albrecht, Karl, *Service Within,* Homewood, IL: Dow Jones-Irwin, 1990.

Ames, B. Charles and James D. Hlavacelc, *Managerial Marketing: The Ultimate Advantage,* Mountainside, NJ: Managerial Marketing, Inc., 1984.

"Big Q at Big Blue," *Quality Progress,* May 1991, pp. 17–21.

Blanchard, Ken, "Communication is the Key to Effective Management," *Today's Office,* June 1991, p. 28.

Bratton, David A., "Organization Challenges of the 1990s: Leadership, Service, Culture, and Morale," *Optimum,* 1989–1990, pp. 75–78.

Clark, Ronald S., "Quality Public Service: the Ottawa-Carleton Experience," *Optimum,* 1990–91, pp. 54–58.

Clemmer, Jim, "The Service/Quality Revolution: An Opportunity for Public Sector Renewal," *Optimum,* 1990–91, pp. 40–51.

Crain, Bob, ''Office Evolution: Tomorrow's Workplace in the Making,'' *AISP Dialogue,* November/December 1988, pp. 4–5, 7.

Davidow, William H. and Bro Uttal, *Total Customer Service,* Harper Perennial, 1989.

Davidson, Jeffrey P., *The Marketing Sourcebook for Small Business,* John Wiley & Sons, Inc., 1989, p. 211.

Dobyns, Lloyd, ''Ed Deming Wants Big Changes, and He Wants Them Fast,'' *Smithsonian,* August 1990, pp. 74–82.

Evans, David, ''The Myth of Customer Service,'' *Canadian Business,* March 1991, pp. 34–39.

''Even Closer to the Customer,'' *Harvard Business Review,* January–February 1991, pp. 9–10.

Farber, Barry and Joyce Wycoff, ''Customer Service: Evolution and Revolution,'' *Sales and Marketing Management,* May 1991, pp. 44–51.

Faulkner, Harold Underwood, *American Political & Social History,* New York: Appleton-Century Crofts, Inc., 1957, pp. 538–539.

Feder, Barnaby J., ''Xerox Plans to Trim 2,500 From White-Collar Staff,'' *The New York Times,* December 12, 1991, p. D3.

Fowler, Elizabeth M., ''Many Banks Are Seeking Help in Sales,'' *The New York Times,* October 29, 1991, p. D21.

Gabor, Andrea, *The Man Who Discovered Quality,* Times Books, Random House, 1990.

Gatlin, Rebecca J. and Kerry P. Gatlin, "Emphasizing Customer Service," *Education Forum,* February 1991, pp. 34–35.

"Getting Started with Telemarketing," AT&T, 1989.

Goodrich, Jonathan N. "Telecommuting in America," *Business Horizons,* July–August 1990, pp. 31–36.

Gordon, Jack, "Where the Training Goes," *Training,* October 1990, pp. 51–69.

Gunderson, Morley, "Implementation of Comparable Worth in Canada," *Journal of Social Issues,* Vol. 45, No. 4, 1989, pp. 209–222.

Hillary, David "Our Quality Really is Job One," *Optimum,* 1990–91, pp. 72–75.

Le Boeuf, Michael, *How to Win Customers and Keep Them for Life,* New York: Berkley Books, 1989, p. 164.

Levitt, Theodore, "Marketing Success Through Differentiation—of Anything," *Harvard Business Review,* January–February 1980, p. 85.

"Making Advertising Pay Off," AT&T, 1989.

Martin, William B., *Managing Quality Customer Service,* Los Altos, CA: Crisp Publications, Inc., 1989, p. 20.

McKenna, Regis, "Marketing is Everything," *Harvard Business Review,* January–February 1991, pp. 66, 68–69.

Ohsann, Tim. "Is Anyone There?" *THINK,* No. 4/1990, p. 41.

Parasuraman, A., Leonard L. Berry and Valarie A. Zeibaml, "Understanding Customer Expectations of Service," *Sloan Management Review,* Spring 1991, p. 39.

Peters, Tom, *Thriving on Chaos,* New York: Harper & Row, 1987, pp. 113–114.

Peters, Tom and Nancy Austin, *A Passion for Excellence,* Warner Books, 1985, pp. 4–6.

"The Quality Imperative," *Business Week,* October 25, 1991.

Rayner, Bruce C.P., "Market-Driven Quality: IBM's Six Sigma Crusade,"*Electronic Business,* October 15, 1990.

Ross, Marilyn and Tom Ross, *Big Marketing Ideas for Small Business,* Homewood, IL: Dow Jones-Irwin, 1990, pp. 163–164.

Schlesinger, Leonard A. and James L. Heskett, "Breaking the Cycle of Failure in Services," *Sloan Management Review,* Spring 1991, pp. 17–20.

Snelling, Robert O. and Anne N. Snelling, *Jobs!* Simon and Schuster, Inc., 1989.

Sobel, Stuart and Gary Hines, "Cray's New Focus on Customers," AFSM International, April 1991, pp. 40–45.

"Social Movements and Problems," *Concise History of the United States,* Oxford Book Company, 1962, p. 240.

"TLC: The Best Employee Motivator," *Working Woman,* October 1991. p. 104.

Townsend, Patrick L. with Joan E. Gebhardt, *Commit to Quality,* New York: John Wiley & Sons, 1990.

United States Department of Labor, *Dictionary of Occupational Titles,* Washington, DC, 1991.

United States Department of Labor, *Occupational Outlook Handbook,* Washington, DC, 1990–91.

Uttal, Bro, "Companies That Serve You Best," *Fortune,* December 7, 1987, p. 98

Verity, John W., Thane Peterson, Deidre Depke, and Evan L. Schwartz, "The New IBM," *Business Week,* December 16, 1991, pp. 112–118.

Wagel, William H. and Hermine Zagat Levine, "HR '90: Challenges and Opportunities," *Personnel,* June 1990, pp. 18–31.

"Work Force 2000: Talk, Talk, Talk," *Training,* May 1991, p. 84.

Yate, Martin John, "To Serve Customers Serve Employees," *Personnel,* December 1990, pp. 15–16.

VGM CAREER BOOKS

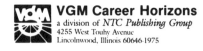

VGM Career Horizons
a division of *NTC Publishing Group*
4255 West Touhy Avenue
Lincolnwood, Illinois 60646-1975